IAN RAMSEY
BISHOP OF DURHAM

A Memoir

Ian and Margaret Ramsey outside Auckland Castle in 1972

IAN RAMSEY
BISHOP OF DURHAM

A Memoir

DAVID L. EDWARDS

LONDON
Oxford University Press
NEW YORK   TORONTO
1973

Oxford University Press, Ely House, London W.1

GLASGOW NEW YORK TORONTO MELBOURNE WELLINGTON
CAPE TOWN IBADAN NAIROBI DAR ES SALAAM LUSAKA ADDIS ABABA
DELHI BOMBAY CALCUTTA MADRAS KARACHI LAHORE DACCA
KUALA LUMPUR SINGAPORE HONG KONG TOKYO

ISBN 0 19 213111 7

Printed in Great Britain
by Northumberland Press Limited
Gateshead

To
Margaret Ramsey
in gratitude

Contents

Preface

WHEN Bishop Ramsey died it was naturally felt that a summary of his life and thought ought to be published. With the agreement of his family, the Oxford University Press accepted the proposal that I should write a short book for publication around the first anniversary of his death. A memoir of this sort is in no way incompatible with later and more expert studies, biographical or philosophical, but even such a limited project could not have been attempted without the assurance of the ready co-operation of Ian Ramsey's colleagues and friends. About two hundred gave me memories and impressions by letter or interview.

For a time, while Editor of the SCM Press, I was one of Ian Ramsey's publishers. Later on he made me one of his examining chaplains and a member of his commission about church life in Sunderland. I was, however, never one of his pupils or closest collaborators, and I am grateful for the help and freedom which have been given me to make this honest assessment.

Westminster Abbey
Easter 1973

D.L.E.

I

The Man We Knew

THE philosopher chosen to be Bishop of Durham in 1966 had been more comfortably placed as an Oxford professor. He became a bishop at a time when the Church of England was facing—or turning away from—many problems. It had largely lost the influence which it had held in the Victorian age, and even as recently as 1945. On the whole the nation, in so far as it thought about the Church at all, probably assumed that most of the Church's problems could not be solved. However, the new bishop had many opportunities, for individual members of the Church of England might still exercise a considerable influence. Usually this influence was local. Lay churchgoers might be respected by colleagues and neighbours as being honest, kind, and hard-working, or the parson would be welcomed as a man dedicated to helping others—however little people might be interested in a priest's religion. The leaders of the Church of England could sometimes gain attention if what they were saying seemed thoughtful and relevant (or controversially sensational). And Ian Thomas Ramsey did gain attention. By seizing his opportunities both in County Durham and nationally, he became not only one of the most influential bishops but also one with a unique appeal.

When he appeared on television no one sounded less like a bishop (as people would say, meaning it as a compliment), but he seemed to embody what remained attractive about the Church. He was obviously a very friendly man, without a trace of the pride or pomp often associated with prelates. The son of a Manchester Post Office worker, he retained a fairly strong Lancashire accent, which appealed to many who reacted against the public school and Oxbridge plumminess of the Anglican leadership. He was a little, tubby man, so that people tended to feel affectionate towards him once they realized that he did not have a chip on his shoulder about being small or overweight or originally under-privileged. But he was bursting with intelligence as well as with goodwill, and seemed to have the energy to tackle any problem.

Although sociologists would locate most of his boyhood inside the middle classes, many people when they saw him in action as a bishop were interested chiefly in the fact that he was not aloof from the working classes. A brigadier speaking at a Conservative dinner referred to him contemptuously as 'the Diddy bishop' (the phrase was familiar from the fussy little Diddy men appearing on the Ken Dodd show on TV), but as a result the bishop found himself the subject of a student demonstration in Durham: 'We love our Diddy bishop.' Because he thought that the pleasures of the working man were being attacked, he defended the night clubs of the North-East against legislation to curb gaming. He was also widely reported as being interested in the religious implications of pop music—and as sympathetically comparing the Beatles' fans with religious worshippers. Like a disc jockey, he linked pop records broadcast on Radio Durham and chosen by exiles from County Durham whom he had met in his travels. The man who organized Radio Durham recalls from the meetings of its advisory council: 'You could always rely on him to come down on one side or the other, usually the side of the working man.' And Ian Ramsey expressed the worries of the working man in the very heart of the Establishment: the House of Lords. Ordinary people felt that he cared.

Intellectuals respected him for other reasons. As one wrote after his death, 'he believed in thinking, which few church leaders seem to do'. Dr. Gordon Wolstenholme, Director of the Ciba Foundation for the promotion of international co-operation in medical and chemical research, collaborated with Ian Ramsey over three years in the discussions which led to the publication of a collection of essays on *Personality and Science* in 1971. He writes:

From the beginning I liked Ian enormously and he made a delightful working colleague without any trace of 'side', intellectual arrogance, condescension, or antagonism, even to people who rather aggressively differed from his own beliefs. I must confess that at first I thought that Ian was almost incomprehensible, impossible to tie down, and using language apparently to confuse rather than to clarify the issues. It very rapidly became clear, however, that any difficulty in following his train of thought was because he was making such a total effort to be scrupulously honest in every single statement he made; as a result, there would be an almost interminable series of parenthetic qualifications to demonstrate that there was no dross on the pure metal of truth which he was assaying.

I came to regard Ian as the touchstone of mental honesty. If you can imagine his rather rotund body tied in knots, he would literally twist himself and pull at his face in the effort to be as absolutely truthful in our discussions as possible. Sometimes this would lead to a startling situation in which this great bishop would seem to be doubting whether he was a Christian at all. There was certainly no artifice or contrivance in this, but it compelled the respect of the scientific members of our group and forced them to reply in equally accurate terms. Ian Ramsey was the least dogmatic man I have ever met in any discipline.

From 1944 to 1966 he taught the philosophy of religion, first as a University Lecturer in Cambridge, then (from 1951) as Nolloth Professor of the Philosophy of the Christian Religion at Oxford. As a young man he had shown ability in mathematics and science, and he always tried to keep in touch with them (rather than with literature or music or the arts). His mind seemed to belong to the modern world. Once when he was being driven from the station to Rochester Cathedral where he was to lecture, he had a few moments of conversation with the driver about bridges. He was interested in their construction, partly because his son Vivian was becoming a civil engineer. He remarked, however, that his own job in life was to build bridges between Christian theology and modern problems. That conversation stayed in the driver's mind, but it might equally well have been about trains—and not only because his son Paul was beginning a career with British Rail. From an early age Ian Ramsey enjoyed the study of time-tables and engines. While Bishop of Durham he made the eight-hour return journey between his home and London at least once every week (with a few exceptions, mainly when he was abroad), and he used to assure people that he enjoyed travelling. Each journey would take him to a meeting to which he looked forward, as others look forward to bed. During a meeting he did not snooze or doodle;

instead it was his habit to make neat notes in his minute writing
about what everyone was saying.

He was greatly admired by many Christians, whether or not
they belonged to the Church of England. Professor John Hick, who
teaches the philosophy of religion in the University of Birmingham,
has written: 'I thought of him as a wonderful person, and a stimulating thinker, and hoped that he would become a great Archbishop of Canterbury.' An experienced journalist who (unlike John
Hick) is an Anglican clergyman has written that Ian Ramsey's
death 'was a devastating blow to the Church of England for not
only had it lost its most able bishop, it had also been deprived of the
only serious contender for the Archbishopric of Canterbury when
Michael Ramsey offered his resignation.'[1] He was often tipped for
Canterbury, and often compared with William Temple, the near-
legendary and still-quoted archbishop whose premature death in
1944 was being felt as a wound a quarter of a century later. In 1968
Ian Ramsey delivered a long and careful lecture on William
Temple, observing that 'people often recall Temple's massive intellect which could interweave the Christian faith and philosophy with
a calm ease and striking clarity. They recall too the outstanding
character of his Christian social concern.'[2] Above all, William
Temple was 'the People's Archbishop' during the second world
war. Those who hoped that Ian Ramsey would become a great
archbishop in the Temple tradition were thinking not only of his
intellectual gifts but also of his popularity. And in the circumstances,
this was a specially great compliment.

William Temple was very much the son of his father, the
Archbishop of Canterbury who had crowned Edward VII, except
that he knew less science than his father did. His mind was
extraordinarily open, but had been formed in all essentials before
post-Keynes economics had become a science dealing with a highly
complex, industrial society, and before post-Russell philosophy had
been revolutionized by the clarifying analysis of language. It was
also the case that the problem of the Church of England had mul-
tiplied with depressing consequences since William Temple's
advocacy of 'life and liberty' for the Church. When tackling the
challenges confronting a diocesan bishop at the turn of the 1960s
and 1970s, Ian Ramsey had to use more energy, flexibility, and

[1] Trevor Beeson, *The Church of England in Crisis* (1973), p. 166.
[2] The lecture was printed in the *Bishoprick* (November 1969).

courage than Temple had needed; and when chairing a commission on Christian doctrine he faced a theological scene more confused than the context of the previous commission, under Temple's chairmanship, between the world wars. If, therefore, anyone hoped that by the 1980s the Church of England under Ian Ramsey's leadership would have formulated a strong message to the new society, and would have recovered its inner confidence, that person would be paying a tribute to Ian Ramsey greater than any truly appropriate to William Temple.

The course of his work as an advocate of Christianity took Ian Ramsey into the storm-centres. For no problems confronting the Christian religion in England were greater than the alienation of scientifically minded intellectuals and the loss of the working classes.

It could be argued that neither the intellectuals nor the workers had ever been very keen on churchgoing. It could also be pointed out that Christian intellectuals and Christian workers existed. Nevertheless the tasks which fell to the lot of Ian Ramsey as a philosophical theologian, and as the bishop of a largely working-class diocese, were immense and, for Christianity's future, vital. The university don's contempt for theology's past claim to be the queen of the sciences had one thing in common with the Durham miner's anger at the past wealth of the bishop and the cathedral. Both reactions expressed the conviction that the Church deserved no high status in a secularized democracy which relied on a science-based technology. The practical atheism of the England in which most of Ian Ramsey's life was spent lay behind what he wrote in his 1971 booklet on *Our Understanding of Prayer*: 'To many people today prayer seems an extraordinary exercise. If the farmer wants a good crop of apples, some would say, is it not more sensible to spray fertilisers than to promote prayers?' Not content with these major tasks related to belief in God, Ian Ramsey made his mark on many subsidiary problems. He was deeply interested in the relevance of Christian morality to ethical issues in medicine, politics, and industry. He was also prominently concerned for the communication of the Christian vision; for education and television. And after leaving Oxford he was involved up to the neck in the modernization of the Church, in his position as fourth in the Church of England's hierarchy, and as the pastor and reformer of a specially problematic diocese.

He was not stupid, and was often daunted by the size of these problems. He was not insensitive, and was often hurt by other men's rejection of what he stood for, whether as a theologian or as a bishop. He was not unaware how many of his fellow-churchmen seemed oblivious of the challenges, or at least incapable of rising to them. Professor Dorothy Emmet, who had several talks with him while he was Bishop of Durham, has written: 'Under his imperturbable demeanour he had a feeling of desperation about the need to rethink the problem of religious truth in a world where our scientific understanding of man, and indeed the understanding of science and philosophy themselves, were changing in ways of which most people in the churches were unaware.' But in public at any rate, he was always optimistic. He would speak of a new Renaissance and a new Reformation as if they were not only desirable but also around the corner. He looked ahead to a new culture combining science and humanity, and to a new civilization. His last words in the House of Lords (on 22 March 1972) were about 'this search for a new culture and this pilgrimage towards a better humanity'.

In part this confidence was due to a good humour which, since it was devoid of self-importance, evoked a positive response from those around him. A Fellow of Christ's remembers from the Cambridge years: 'In a college noted for the acidity of the remarks of some of the Fellows, particularly concerning ecclesiastics, I never heard an ill word spoken of Ian. Never once!' 'He was invariably good company', another Cambridge colleague remarked. 'He was, so far as I could see, universally liked, which amounts to no easy achievement in a small and often rather introspective society. He was on excellent terms with people who didn't like clergymen on principle.'

In a memorial address in the university church at Oxford, Basil Mitchell (his successor as Nolloth Professor) recalled Professor Ramsey. 'He had pre-eminently the gift of encouraging other people to make their own distinctive contribution to a co-operative enterprise. And any enterprise on which he was engaged became a co-operative one. . . . He was fond of describing, by way of illustration, how a stiff and formal party suddenly comes alive; "the ice is broken" and "disclosures" begin to occur. He must often have had occasion to observe this, for it was just the effect his own presence at a party was likely to have.'

'The fact of the matter was that he was a class (at least) above the rest of us', Sir Derman Christopherson, F.R.S., Vice-Chancellor of Durham, has written, adding about a royal visit to Durham Cathedral on Maundy Thursday 1967: 'Without making the occasion any less grand, Ian domesticated it. It is impossible to decide how he did it except by his own supreme naturalness. That is an art we should all of us like to have.' A similar memory is contributed by 'Kit' Robinson, the former General Secretary of the Durham Miners' Association:

He never talked down to people, having the happy knack of reaching individuals at their own level. He was very interested in youth welfare, and he seemed to have a remarkable ability to reach out and talk to youngsters who were sometimes difficult to understand. This outreach was evidenced in many other ways. I recall that two of the speakers chosen for our 1971 gala were unable to come and our Executive Committee mandated me to ask Ian Ramsey if he would, at short notice, take the place of one of them. Perhaps some people were surprised—after all, never before had we had a bishop as a speaker on Durham Miners' Gala Day. I am sure Ian was one of the most popular speakers ever to speak from a Big Meeting platform. I have yet to meet a person who has criticised our late bishop in any way. He was truly a man of the people.

However, this ebullience and friendliness were clearly connected with a religious faith. For him, this did not mean a cosmic complacency. On the contrary his *Christian Discourse* (1965) made clear his belief that 'the Church, like the universities, when each is faithful to its vision, is amongst the few institutions in the universe which must display divine dissatisfaction with things as they are.' But no one who heard the prayers which he took such trouble to select or to compose for use in church, or who saw him on his knees in a chapel silent before he celebrated a service of Holy Communion, could doubt that he was a man of prayer. There was a calm at the centre of the dissatisfaction. He was commonly regarded, even before his death, as a saint: as one whose life helps others to believe in God. The hymn 'For all the saints' was sung at his consecration as a bishop in York Minster because this happened to be All Saints' Day 1966. It was sung at some of the memorial services after his death for more personal reasons.

An advanced Anglo-Catholic congregation in Sunderland—unvisited by the previous Bishop of Durham because its worship was so much higher than the authorized forms of common prayer—was delighted when he 'pontificated' at High Mass (after a much needed rehearsal) and shook each one of them by the hand with a word of cheer. Members of that congregation were not alone in comparing this holy, humble man with Pope John XXIII. After his death, Ian Ramsey's memory was used by more than one preacher as a parable about the Fatherhood of God. 'Surely everyone who met him must remember that most fatherly characteristic,' one parish priest in his diocese said, 'how he came out towards them, not only in the warmth of his personality and the genuineness of his interest, but very often physically as well. It was not in him to stand and wait for people to come to him, to stand on the dignity which was surely his. His heart went out to them and that short and energetic figure responded, getting up from his desk, out of his car, his hand outstretched, all interest, all concern, no discrimination, no holding back—a father indeed.'

His life's work, while it touched on many problems, was basically always an attempt to communicate this religion. One of his favourite quotations was from A. N. Whitehead's *Science and the Modern World*. 'Religion is the vision of something which stands beyond, behind, and within the passing flux of immediate things, something which is real, and yet waiting to be realized, something which is a remote possibility and yet the greatest of present facts, something whose possession is the final good, and yet is beyond reach: something which is the ultimate ideal and the hopeless quest.' But in his own teaching, he would speak of *Someone* rather than *something*, and he would not say that the quest was 'hopeless'. His discovery of God coloured his use of another Whitehead quotation. 'That religion is strong which in its ritual and its modes of thought evokes an apprehension of the commanding vision. The worship of God is not a rule of safety—it is an adventure of the spirit, a flight after the unattainable. The death of religion comes with the repression of the high hope of adventure.'

He often spoke of 'commitment' after 'discernment'. These were the two principal themes which he had picked out of the philosophy of Joseph Butler, Bishop of Durham, 1750-2. Butler pointed out that an estimate of 'probability' remains far from certain, but 'in matters of practice, will lay us under an absolute and formal obligation'; and he illustrated this from the obligation felt by a man to jump in the river in order to save a drowning child, although there is no certainty of either rescue or survival. The other theme from Bishop Butler developed by Bishop Ramsey concerns the human condition. When we think, we know ourselves to be more than 'gross bodies'; and we can be led by reasonable reflection to consider 'this little scene of human life, in which we are so busily engaged, as having a reference of some sort or other, to a much larger plan of things'. The adventure to which these two Bishops of Durham summoned their sceptical contemporaries was a moral commitment in daily action, based on the discernment that a person—even a drowning child—is ultimately more than the details of bodily behaviour: more truly personal, and eternally more significant in the universe.[1]

So God was approached through morality. But it was clear to Ramsey's more perceptive hearers that (although he lacked the eloquence, and even the wish, to describe any mystical experience of his own) he had a sense of the divine glory which went beyond the stern imperative of duty. When concluding his lectures in 1960 at the Queen's University, Belfast, later published under the title *Religion and Science: Conflict and Synthesis*, he expressed a long-standing admiration for a philosopher and bishop who was a contemporary of Joseph Butler's: the Irishman, George Berkeley, Bishop of Cloyne, 1734-53. He also preached an immense sermon to Trinity College, Dublin, about Berkeley, two hundred years after his death.

Berkeley, as summarized by Ramsey, said in effect: 'We see God as we see persons. Hair, face, skin, all these are visible, but to "see" a *person* is to see these, and more besides. Likewise God. We look on the universe, from galaxies to mesons, from blood sugar to insulin, from points to entropy, from acetic acid to vitamin B, from hydrogen to whatever element at the moment closes the periodic table, and by and through them all we see God as we see a person, through his hair and face and skin—a person who is all these and more. The world, as Berkeley taught us to look on it, is divine, visual language, and all we need to add some two hundred years later is that what the scientist does and what the theologian does, each in his own way, is to discover the logical patterns of this divine visual language as best he can.'

Many were surprised by the confidence with which Ian Ramsey placed himself in the tradition of Bishops Butler and Berkeley, for

[1] A lecture by Ian Ramsey on *Joseph Butler* was published by Dr. Williams's Library, London, in 1969.

in Ramsey's lifetime man was more usually regarded as a naked ape thrown up by evolution, and ultimately as a biochemical freak. Man's freedom was more generally interpreted as a brave (although doomed) defiance of a restricting social code and of a hostile or indifferent environment. The universe was more widely thought to be the language not of God but of randomness and of inexplicable space. And during his lifetime Ramsey did not usually succeed in conveying his vision to sceptics, partly because he was reluctant to speak about his own experience. He was not always cerebral; when taking church services or delivering devotional addresses, he was open to the criticism that he was sentimental. But he preferred to express his faith in an unemotional tone, as befitted a mathematician who had become a philosopher. This made his faith, during an age of such widespread scepticism, puzzling.

Another puzzle which many recognized as they looked back on his life was why he had killed himself by overwork. This was probably not the only cause of his death; he was overweight, and his life may have been shortened both by a serious illness as a young man and by a severe attack of food-poisoning in 1969, while at a conference. But his habit of overworking demands some notice.

He was a transparently good man, but also a bravely honest one, and in telling his story it is our duty to avoid what he once called 'epitaph extravagance'. In *Religious Language* (1957) he discussed how the word 'perfect' is used about God although we cannot claim to have met a perfect man. He used two bishops to illustrate his argument. Bishop Z is a most competent administrator and also a saint, 'but a perfect man would be a better bishop'.

Then we think of B, who is not only a saint, a good administrator, has all the qualities of the 'perfect' bishop—friendly, cheerful, and human, with a strong sense of pastoral duty and so on. But people will say, B may be all that, but he is not 'devout'. It will then be retorted: how can he fail to be 'devout' if he is a 'saint'? And the conversation will now begin to fix on senses of sanctity which might not imply 'being devout', and so on. The story will have to go on until, at one and the same time, there dawns on us the futility of ever hoping to get a cut-and-dried description of 'perfection', and a situation was evoked which somehow or other presented to us the 'perfection', the 'ideal', after which we were searching.

His own physically fatal defect was, however, not mentioned in that passage. His chief limitation was that he did not insist on priorities. He lacked a sense of discrimination or proportion when responding to what he saw as need. While a bishop he had such a horror of being merely an official that he went to the opposite extreme and threw himself wholeheartedly into far too much.

The tendency he was fighting against was illustrated seven years before he went to Durham by a remark he made during a philosophical gathering, when he was discussing behaviour which was less than personal. 'Someone might ask the bishop, "Who preached the sermon last week?" And he might answer, "*The bishop preached*". Very true, because it had been a very official, prelatical, impersonal sermon, so that people said, "Just like the bishop's purple self".'[1] But instead of conserving his energies by sticking to an official role, he lavished them on every person and every cause claiming his attention. He drove himself mercilessly. He rose early and went to bed late, and when awake seldom rested his mind. His recreation was to change his preoccupation. In theory he knew how necessary it is to relax; he put 'family and home' as the first of his recreations in *Who's Who*, was eloquent about the pleasures of cycling and walking, and often urged his clergy to make sure of good holidays and a regular day off. But particularly while he was a bishop, somehow in his own case some duty always had to be done urgently. Years of overwork and of continuous stress contributed to two severe heart attacks in 1972. He died after the second, eight to a dozen years before he would normally have retired.

Naturally people thought of his death as a tragedy which had deprived Church and State of a leader at the height of his powers. The fact was, however, that his acceptance of many distractions from his main tasks had already gravely damaged his work, both as a philosopher and as a bishop.

His philosophical work was never brought to public completion. His books consisted of printed lectures, and as Don Cupitt observed in a review in *Theology* (June 1964): 'As so often in reading his books one is impressed by the author's range, his style, and his ingenuity, but one is left asking for a more extended treatment.' That Ian Ramsey would have granted the justice of this complaint may be seen from his preface to *Religious Language* (his first book). 'To some, a game may provide all the reason we need for accepting its rules; others, less easily satisfied, may ask for an independent

[1] *Prospect for Metaphysics*, ed. I. T. Ramsey (1961), p. 165.

and altogether more philosophical discussion of my starting-point.
These die-hards will, I hope, look sometime in another book which
I hope soon to publish under the title *Fact, Metaphysics and God*.'
When he died fifteen years later, however, he had written no more
than the first draft of this projected *magnum opus*.[1] His lectures
on *Religious Language* will therefore always remain his most comprehensive published work. He wrote a great deal else, as the
present short book will mention, and his filing cabinets were
stuffed with notes for lectures and talks. But he never built a
system, developing his insights at leisure and defending them
against the attacks or misunderstandings which they invited.

The damage done to his work as a bishop by his lack of a sense
of priority or proportion will be shown later. Here it will be enough
to note that many of his clergy, including those who loved and
respected him most, were really puzzled by his behaviour; for he
seemed to regard being a pastorally active and administratively
creative Bishop of Durham as a half-time job. He did not have
the time to think through and unify the necessary reforms, or to
prepare for and consolidate such advances as took place, or to arouse
the goodwill and energy of slow-moving people. He obviously
enjoyed his visits to parishes and homely chats with clergy and
people, and knew from many expressions of gratitude how deeply
they were appreciated, but he also knew how necessary it was to
give the impression that he had all the time in the world for a
worried individual or a troublesome problem; yet the plain fact,
which he made every effort to conceal, was that he did not have
the time. 'My one wish is that throughout the diocese—with laity
as well as clergy—I am known to be accessible to anyone at any
time.' So he wrote a few months before his death. But it was
impossible; he was too often away. His admirers asked each other
why he did not give himself more of a chance to become a
thoroughly effective bishop in his diocese, before moving on to
make that impact on the national life which only an Archbishop of
Canterbury can make.

It is, however, by no means certain that, had he lived, he would
have become Archbishop of Canterbury. A proposal to appoint
him would certainly have been resisted behind the scenes by some
on theological and by others on political grounds, for although

---

[1] It contains longer treatments of the logics of Russell and Carnap, and of the
nature of religious experience, than are to be found in the published work.

his temperament was eirenic his integrity was such that he never hid his rejection of religious or political conservatism. On most of the topics of the day he had views to offer, and most of his views were liberal. This inevitably led some to protest that he ought to have stayed out of controversy, and others to feel that he did not really appreciate the strength of the conservative position. Whether because of the numerical strength of conservatives among the clergy and regular churchgoers, or if a Conservative Prime Minister had had the chief say in the choice of the next Archbishop of Canterbury, these hesitations on the ground of Ian Ramsey's radicalism might well have been decisive. On the other hand, it is equally possible that such hesitations might have been over-ruled had the Prime Minister and the others responsible for advising the Crown on the appointment been conscientious in seeking the man who would lead the Church best—and had Ian Ramsey been that man beyond dispute. We may say: no doubt the appointment would have been handled conscientiously. It is not nearly so clear that Ian Ramsey's temperamental suitability to be Archbishop of Canterbury would have seemed obvious to every conscience, and an issue also in doubt for theological or political reasons might have been settled by a lack of confidence about the personal element.

Trevor Beeson, after paying him the tribute already quoted, has written: 'In retrospect it can be seen that even had Ian Ramsey gone to Canterbury a man of his temperament, who could never decline an invitation, would have been unable to survive the constant pressures of the office.' A good many people saw this danger while Ian Ramsey was alive, and warned him. A bishop recalls:

I remember one day walking back from Lambeth to Westminster with him, and feeling sufficiently senior to express my mind to him. I told him that we all had the highest hopes of what he was capable of giving to the Church of England, and hoped that he would be given the opportunity of the highest office, but that it was obvious to us all that if he carried on as he was doing, he would kill himself. He made some sympathetic reply, but did not change his ways.

One reason why he did not change was that he was not governed by ambition or vanity. He knew for what reasons many placed the highest hopes in him. But when friends occasionally ventured to ask him how he reacted to the frequent talk in church circles that his destiny lay in Canterbury, he would reply that he was absorbed in his existing duties and opportunities; and people believed him.

They were confirmed in their belief when he seemed to go out of his way to risk offending Mr. Heath, who became the Conservative Prime Minister in 1970. He led a deputation to Downing Street in order to protest against the sale of arms to South Africa, and attacked the Industrial Relations Bill in the House of Lords. He realized that he was publicly touching two highly delicate areas in current politics, but had not made complete preparations to equip himself for the controversies. He was not unequipped; he had studied the facts and pondered the moral issues, and he carefully avoided the extravagant sentimentalities of some of those who looked to him for a moral lead. He was, however, not impregnable. He was open to a detailed rejoinder from the Prime Minister, and to a charge from the next speaker in the Lords (Lord Thorneycroft) that his idealism was inappropriate when debating legislation. But to Ian Ramsey it was not an agonizing problem, whether or not he should bear witness when he had his chance in Downing Street and Parliament. He was doing his duty.

Most of this was, from most points of view, an admirable example of the industrious spirit of Lancashire; of pastoral care, at the service of all; and of moral courage. The Headmaster of his school in the 1930s, Mr. Wilson, wrote after his death: 'My predecessor (Mr. McCarter) said that he could not understand why Ramsey was so popular, in spite of the fact that he always stood for the right. Perhaps it was because he stood for the right—and he was no prig. I think that later on he was a "bishop" in the fullest and widest sense of the word. He would undertake whatever he was physically capable of doing for any person or community. I think Christ's instruction *Feed my lambs* was ever Ian's watchword.'

But there still remains for many of those who look back on his life the puzzle as to why Ian Ramsey allowed it to be so fragmentary, as to why he allowed it to be cut short, and as to why so much had to be sacrificed to his sense of duty. He was so often warned against doing too much that it must have been yet another test of his patience and self-control to give the stock, polite answer. His own family and personal staff added their entreaties and were reassured, but the style of life continued. In the last weeks of his life, some of those who met him in action had what one of them has called a 'chill fear'. He assured his friends after his first heart attack that he had learned his lesson, but they saw that he had not. In his last weeks he was adding to his duties by pressing ahead with a group to study euthanasia (when others thought there was nothing fresh to say) and by leading the formation of an inquiry by the Social Morality Council into broadcasting and television. His friends had to face with dismay the truth that he had become a compulsive worker, and it seemed inexplicably irrational. One of the psychiatrists among his friends has spoken of Ian Ramsey being 'trapped' in this self-imposed cage of overwork. One of his brother-bishops has written that 'some demon seemed to be driving him'.

After his death, some blamed the Church for imposing too many duties on him. It would appear, however, that no one can regulate a bishop's duties except the bishop himself. It must be for him to pronounce the essential word, 'no'. Those who organize services, meetings, and committees cannot be expected to refrain from wanting a bishop—at least, not when the bishop is a man such as Ian Ramsey. Consequently the bishops of the Church of England have been inundated with invitations—at least, since Samuel Wilberforce, the great Victorian Bishop of Oxford, set a new standard of episcopal activity and talkativeness—and the more popular and conscientious bishops have been the more tempted to do and say too much. Archbishop Randall Davidson complained about the young William Temple: 'The trouble with dear William is, he is so kind he cannot say "no".' After William Temple's death, F. R. Barry, then Bishop of Southwell, wrote: 'He was everywhere, unspared and unsparing, constantly travelling up and down the country.... It killed him. Is the Church so rich in prophets that it can afford to squander the gifts of God?' But partly because his base for a national and international operation was some 250 miles from London, in County Durham where he tried to maintain a close grip on local problems, Ian Ramsey's diary was even fuller and less sensible than Archbishop Temple's.

C. P. Snow, who was on affectionate terms with him from the days when he was his tutor at Cambridge to the days when they both sat in the Lords, has written: 'I mustn't pretend that I knew him intimately. I sometimes doubted whether anyone did. Un-assuming and outgoing as he was, there was something ungraspable about his character.' Gordon Fallows, Bishop of Sheffield, who was Principal of Ripon Hall, Oxford, when Professor Ramsey lived there with his family, and who then and later knew him 'fairly well', has written: 'He was indeed an enigmatic character.'

Many of us who came across Ian Ramsey in one or more of his innumerable activities would agree with a Roman Catholic layman (Edward Oliver) that 'it was difficult not to think of oneself as his friend from the first moment that one met him. He had a *charisma*, that intelligence of the heart which is much more than mere amiability.' Another of his countless friends has written of his 'rare gift of instant communication'. But for all that, he was a mystery. We did not know all that he did or was. Nor did we understand why he did and was so much. It was not only that he was almost always throughout his life too busy for a gossip or for an exchange of confidences. It was also that he did not seem to wish to dramatize or even to reveal the self at the heart of the incessant activity. One of his chief interests was in dialogue and co-operation between doctors and clergy, yet he never discussed why he was ruining his own health. His philosophy was built around the importance of the personal, yet he disliked any attempt to analyse emotions deeply. Nor was it easy even for friends skilled in psychology to classify or penetrate his temperament. He was a metaphysician, yet never absent-minded, always fascinated by practical details; a leader with a strong will and a tendency to repeat his own jargon, yet always eager to hear about the interests and the problems of the person with whom he was talking; an elated, over-active man, yet not 'manic'—for there seemed to be no compensating depressions, and his arguments were (or at least, seemed to Christians to be) usually reasonable and down-to-earth.

'I see him as a person whose dominating intellect was illuminated by emotional warmth to an unusual degree, but who was exceptionally reserved in his inner being.' So Dr. Kenneth Soddy, his collaborator in the Institute of Religion and Medicine, writes. And that sums it up. Despite our admiration and love, despite all that he said and wrote and did, we did not know the secret of his vision, and we did not understand why it was driving him to a premature death. We must see if we can understand now. Obviously not all can be discovered—or, a year after his death, told—but it may now be possible to understand a little more about this man whom we knew and did not know.

2

A Disclosure to a Boy

'THERE was always something boyish about him.' So an Oxford colleague recalls. Perhaps it was meant as a casual criticism, but it opens up the whole of Ian Ramsey.

While he was Bishop of Durham he loved no activity more than his annual party for the cathedral choristers. 'In all the games the bishop himself was the starter, handicapper, and judge', the headmaster reports. 'It was this understanding of the boys that so endeared him to them, and they were perfectly at home with him.' It is a far cry to the episcopal splendours of Durham from the nondescript urban sprawl around Bolton where the chief features are the mines, the Exide battery works, and the Pilkington tile factory—from the little red-brick terraced house, 9 Ivy Grove, Kearsley, where he was born on 31 January 1915, or from the semi-detached 366 Manchester Road, Clifton, which they called St. Kilda and which was his home for most of his boyhood. It was literally a move from a cottage to a castle. But his mother moved with him to Auckland Castle in 1966 (when his father had just died), and the psychological truth is that he never ceased to be devoted to his parents and their values. When people marvelled how much he noticed the obscure individual and took trouble to help, they implied another fact: that he had not forgotten what it felt like to be a child in humble circumstances, never asking for sweets or a toy. When people were surprised that he was so outspoken with his left-wing views, they ought to have taken note of what he often said: that he had not forgotten the depression and unemployment of the area where he had grown up. And when people wondered at his confidence, they were pointing to another of the deepest realities in his life. He was the only child of his parents. They adored him and his progress became their chief interest. He enjoyed a privilege which, as Freud observed, is worth considerably more than a fortune: he was utterly secure in his mother's love.

His father worked in the Post Office, and while his father was in the Army during the first world war his mother also helped with the post. When Ian was very young, she would arrange for him to be taken for a walk in the afternoon. But he much preferred trotting out with her round Kearsley delivering the post, or sitting under her desk on a ledger, silently playing with his trains or looking at books. His mother remembers that he could not speak until he was three, but then advanced quickly, being able to watch the clock on behalf of the 'baby' class in his first term at the primary school run by St. John's church. It was the first sign of his mental strength which to some extent he inherited from his father. (Arthur Ramsey, the son of a fitter in Bolton of Scottish descent, began work as a messenger boy delivering telegrams at a penny a time. He was Postmaster of Rochdale in the 1930s, and ended up as Postmaster of Norwich. He was a gentle but immensely thorough man, who loved gardening.) But Ian's dogged, driving energy, like his small stature, came from his mother, Mary Ramsey, and from her Lancashire mining family.

It seems that at school Ian was at first very much mother's boy. A long time later he remembered with indignation that parents were not welcomed at the school; he mentioned it in a House of Lords debate. His mother remembers: 'Ian would not go out to play with the other children but walked about with the teachers. He never had time for play.' But he was not self-centred. One winter's day his mother was worried because he had no overcoat. A teacher told her: 'Mrs. Ramsey, you'll find it on Dan Neery.' Ian explained that Dan was so cold that he had given him the coat. (Years later Dan, who was then working on the Manchester buses, gave Ian a free ride.)

It also seems that, although he was born into a part of Lancashire where most people were strictly respectable and (when employed) hard-working, from an early age he was extraordinarily conscientious. His mother recalls: 'We had family prayers every evening and then I read Ian a story. One story was about playing the game. He had not gone to bed one night when he ought to, and he became very worried that he had not been playing the game. He was always worrying in case he trespassed.' His father's mother, who lived with them, is still remembered as sitting, an old Scottish lady in a chair, with the Bible. Ian Ramsey's acute sense of morality was inevitably linked with the Christian religion. There was of course a strain about this, but it showed only in occasional outbursts of anger. Usually these outbursts came when he thought that some authority was being unreasonably strict.

He went as a scholarship boy to Farnworth Grammar School (co-educational and partly fee-paying) at the age of ten, one year younger than the normal age of entry. Concentrating first on Latin, his mind grew and after two years he was first in his form. (In 1928 he even won the first prize in the sack race.) One of his teachers, Alice Ashcroft, remembers Ian Ramsey sitting in the midst of the class, two at a desk. 'His owl-like appearance and the fact that his eyes never left my face made me find out his name.' But he developed faster as he discovered science. He gained 'distinctions' in what would now be his O levels in pure mathematics and physics as well as in English and Latin, and in what would now be his A levels in pure and applied mathematics and chemistry, with good marks in physics. He became secretary of the scientific society and head prefect. He was hopeless at games, but arranged the school fixtures with zeal. He enjoyed long cycling tours, often with his father, in the holidays. Another of his teachers, May Rankin, reflects: 'Although Ian's achievements were exceptional, they were the result of sheer hard work combined with the desire for understanding and accuracy in all that he undertook. It is greatly to the credit of his parents that their only child although clever was not spoiled or conceited.' It is also greatly to the credit of this school that it placed a good education within a tram-ride of Ramsey's home.

He won a scholarship tenable at Manchester University, but his school's ambition for him now went as far as Cambridge, where eventually he won a place at Christ's College—then a very notable adventure from Farnworth Grammar School. He could afford to take this place up because he also won what was in October 1933 the rare privilege of a State Scholarship plus a major scholarship from Lancashire County Council. His aim was to become a mathematical physicist, or alternatively to enter the higher civil service.

He had attended Sunday School at St. Anne's, Clifton; his teacher was a miner, Tommy Marsh, still alive with a great character in 1973—with whom (as with the grammar school staff) he always kept in touch. He had been confirmed in 1931. (He was struck by the address given by the Bishop of Middleton, Dr. Parsons, with its quotation: 'I know the stars are there—they don't know I'm here.') Through all this he had become friends with the vicar, Trevor Wright. But when he went to Cambridge he was not particularly interested in theology or the Church. Indeed, he was so much the swot wrapped up in his mathematics, and so shy among the public school boys with his smallness and his thick Lancashire accent, that at first he was lonely. He was also very conscious of the need to economize. His expenses were kept at £150 a year, although it was normally reckoned that the minimum was £220. (His accounts were exact, and at the end of each term he gave them to Mum and Dad with a present.) He lived in remote lodgings and failed to eat properly. He neglected a cold which turned into bronchitis and weakened him for tuberculosis. In March 1934, at the age of nineteen, he was sent to the Papworth Sanitorium.

During eight months in hospital and his convalescence, many things happened to Ian Ramsey. He gained his gratitude to doctors, and his interest in their problems. He began to read widely, including some philosophy and theology. He developed his affection for the Church. The Chaplain of Christ's (H. F. Woolnough), hearing of his plight, both visited him and arranged for fellow-undergraduates to do the same. Among these were a number of ordinands; Christ's had Tancred Studentships for those seeking Anglican ordination. In response to such visits, Ramsey poured out his natural friendliness—and more. Several times in his published work he was to refer to the joys of mathematics. 'If we see a billiard ball and talk of $x^2 + y^2 + z^2 = C^2$ we link talk about the billiard ball with talk about oranges, about the earth, about an Association (but not a Rugby) football, about tennis balls, squash balls, raindrops, and suet dumplings.'[1] But he always added a point about the limits to the generalizing power possessed by mathematics and scientific theory. The redness of the sunset is more than the vibrations of colourless point particles. Other people

[1] *Prospect for Metaphysics*, pp. 154-5.

are more than objects, for 'I come to myself' in relations with others. What was involved in such experience? One thing that was clear was that here was a reality coming after physics. 'Metaphysics', he wrote, 'arises from man's desire to know, in a world of change and transitoriness, just where he is journeying; it arises whenever man seeks to map the universe and to plot his position in it'—to answer Kant's three questions, 'What can I know? What ought I to do? What may I hope?'[1]

Above all, in the Papworth Sanitorium Ian Ramsey was given back his life, and it is clear from what he said and wrote at the time that he regarded his recovery as a sign of the loving kindness of God. To his new-found friends he expressed what one of them has recalled as 'the first youthful rapture of his spiritual awakening'. Years later in more sophisticated language he would speak of the universe itself being disclosed as in a personal relationship with the individual.

This explains why his Oxford inaugural lecture was to be on miracles. And it explains something else. Shirley Freeman, a fellow-student who planned to be ordained and who kept a diary, wrote in it: '*6 June 1934.* I was delighted to hear that Ian has chosen the same calling as myself.' And almost forty years later he has written that the reason why Ian Ramsey so often in later life found it impossible to say 'no' to invitations is to be found in this little-known period. 'It was as though his life, unexpectedly put at jeopardy, had been restored to him, and had become a gift which he must ever after use as fully and completely as he was able.' And use for the benefit of others. Alex Wedderspoon has shrewdly commented that 'sincere and outgoing concern' was 'the one feature common to all his multifarious activities in the 1960s, the quality that he managed to communicate to people in all walks of life from miners to peers'.

A Cambridge university sermon by Ramsey in 1949 was for a moment self-disclosing. 'The greatest possible blunder is to interpret conversion in terms of the emotional upheaval of the isolated individual. Conversion is essentially a story about God, with consequences for man; it is not club-room autobiography. If conversion means that we are the subjects of God's redeeming love and grace, we shall never expect to enter into any easy land of plain morality— only into a land which, however lovely, is shadowed by a cross. We

[1] *Ibid.*, p. 153.

are called as converted to no moral peace but in service and suffering
to find our lives.'

Ahead lay many difficulties. He could not resume his university
course until October 1935. Five years later he still had to go to bed
with a cup of cocoa every evening at nine. But he was finding his
life. Shirley Freeman writes: 'I never knew him afterwards ever to
express any doubts about the reality of the call.' Ramsey would
probably have regained his self-confidence anyway, from the academic successes which were now to be his: a First in the Mathematics Tripos Part I in 1936, and another First in Moral Science
(philosophy) Part IIa in 1938. But Bishop T. S. Garrett is indicating
a greater change than this when he writes: 'I confess that I found
myself cycling out to the Papworth Sanitorium rather as a duty....
When I got to know him, his letters to me were naïve and effu-
sive.... Our ways parted after Cambridge, mine to India. I was
surprised when on leave soon after the war to find him developed in
personality out of all recognition.'

At a meeting in October 1936 of one of the college societies (the
Ridout), when a paper on some theological topic had been read,
Ramsey made a brief comment, for the first time. The Master, Dr.
Charles Raven, who was also Regius Professor of Divinity, was
present. Shirley Freeman writes: 'I can see now the look on Canon
Raven's face, expressive of surprise and keen interest, as he turned
swiftly in his chair and followed Ian's words.' So began another of
the formative influences, summed up when Ramsey wrote the
memoir of Raven in the *Proceedings* of the British Academy (1965).
Raven was a theologian passionately concerned that religion and
science should be reconciled. Ramsey put it that Raven sought 'a
new Reformation based on the broad reasonableness of a natural
piety'. He had his reservations about Raven, as others did. In his
memoir he was perceptive about a 'sense of loneliness when appreciation meant much, and where criticism could be peculiarly
wounding'. But it was Charles Raven, more than anyone else, who
made Ian Ramsey's religion adult; who helped to bring his head
and his heart, his science and his piety, closer together, nearer a
single vision.

His main supervisor in philosophy was A. C. Ewing, whose
interests as expressed in his book *Idealism: A Critical Survey* (1934)
were reflected immaturely in Ramsey's own Burney Prize Essay in
1938. A specimen of the style then thought desirable may be given

from the preface to this essay. 'I consider myself least dependent on others in making Space and Time the principles by which abstractions of the experiential unity are made, and in arguing for the Ultimacy of the Volitional Unity, with the consequent corollary of the relative inadequacy of *both* "Supernatural" and Natural concepts. The Supernatural is not the "most Real" we know; the phrase can properly be applied only to the Volitional Unity as an Unabstracted, Concrete Whole.'

More to the point, Ramsey secured the money necessary to pursue his studies by election as Burney Student. This enabled him to gain a third First, this time with distinction (a brilliant achievement), in the philosophical section of the Theological Tripos Part II. Then he crossed over to Oxford; where he was to prepare for ordination at Ripon Hall. This theological college out on Boar's Hill was presided over by H. D. A. Major, controversially modernist in his religion, conservative in his politics and in many of his ways.

Ramsey in no sense dominated his contemporaries in Ripon Hall, but his outstanding abilities were recognized together with his very strong will in things small and great. He was affectionately nicknamed 'Panda' and elected senior student. His first sermon was on the theme: 'Why be religious—isn't it enough to be good?' He was both, alarmingly so; Dr. Major used to recall the exact punctuality with which Ramsey would ring the bells for chapel and meals. One day he went for a walk with Hugh Joseph, who asked him what he hoped to do. The reply was that after some years as a curate he hoped to return to Christ's. 'I think that my ambition, Hugh, would be this: to try to build a bridge between theology and philosophy.'

Dr. C. H. Dodd recalls that Ramsey told him in 1938 that he wanted a spell in Oxford, because the new kind of anti-metaphysical philosophy flourished there. 'Ramsey considered that the challenge that religious propositions were nonsense should be taken up. His hope was that by working himself in the new philosophy he would be able to construct a new apologetic for Christianity taking account of all that they were saying, employing their methods but showing their presuppositions up as arbitrary—a notable example of a man setting himself to prepare the role he was to fulfil.'

But first there had to be a curacy as a 'title' for ordination by Bishop Kenneth Kirk of Oxford. He did not go far from Ripon

Hall—only to Headington Quarry, a village fast becoming a suburb of Oxford. The vicar was T. E. Bleiben, a scholar and friend.

Ramsey lived in the Vicarage and threw himself into wartime parish work, particularly into the St. Christopher's Guild for young people. He wore everyone else's pullovers when playing in goal at a soccer match; and wore almost nothing when playing an Ancient Briton in a pageant. This guild provided the teachers for the Sunday School, and Ramsey's essay for the Bishop of Oxford before ordination as a priest was on Sunday Schools. It was both clever and silly, advocating much higher intellectual standards, to be achieved by closer links between Sunday School teachers and the universities and even by State inspection for efficiency. His own study, where he used to discuss with a dozen boys after Evensong on a Sunday, was strewn with books and piles of papers.

His character was now formed. Peter Lloyd, who was one of those boys, recalls: 'His interest in the person with whom he was talking was so intense that all else was forgotten at that moment; yet this in no way stemmed the ceaseless activity of his intellect, so that one became aware that he was grappling with a number of problems at the same time. One soon experienced also his meticulous attention to detail in whatever he undertook. Those taking part in a parish play would all receive notes of reminder in that tiny handwriting.'

He fell in love with a girl in the parish, Margretta (usually Margaret) McKay from Coleraine near Londonderry. She came into his life because she was so good with the boils from which he suffered. She stayed there until the end. Ian Ramsey wrote in his memoir of Charles Raven: 'There must be a proper reticence about what most clearly touches the heart.' That instruction is to be obeyed, but it may be said that two things become obvious about this marriage. The first was that the reliance he could place on her in caring for the home and the children made it possible for him to give himself to many—no doubt, as time went on, too many— duties away from home. The second was that in his teaching he often spoke about marriage. 'There is no subject of such profound importance and general interest as marriage', he wrote in 1952. But he would particularly stress that the love which may have a physical or even chemical origin can deepen into the love which is an enduring loyalty.

He returned to Christ's in 1943, at the age of twenty-eight, as Chaplain. Next year he became a Fellow, and Director of Studies in Theology and Moral Science. He remained a Fellow until 1951, although he exchanged the Chaplaincy for a Tutorship in 1949. In 1944 he also became a University Lecturer in Divinity—and the 'Canon Ramsey' he remained until 1966, as a Canon Theologian of Leicester Cathedral.

Christ's was not an easy situation. (It is generally assumed that C. P. Snow had not forgotten every aspect of life in that college when he wrote fiction such as *The Light and the Dark* and *The Masters*.) One problem for Ramsey was that there was a war on. As Master, Raven attracted to Christ's a number of undergraduates who shared his pacifism. This gave some of the more patriotic dons a fresh reason for criticizing him. The new Chaplain was in a quiet way a pacifist; but he tactfully avoided being a mere echo to the Master, and always listed in *Who's Who* the appointment which he had held as College ARP and Fire Officer, 1943-5. Someone—not one of the dons, for very few of them ever went to chapel —has said that hearing Ramsey preach after Raven was somewhat like Bach after Wagner. Above all, Ramsey set himself to heal or ignore all personal breaches. Dr. Eric Stokes recalls: 'His ability to enter sympathetically into the personalities of that diversity of creatures making up a college was outstanding. He seemed to know everyone by name, and never forgot a face. He always had a moment to pass a word, but was always in a hurry. If Aristotle was right to define happiness as "satisfying activity", Ramsey was one of the happiest men I have known.'

Maurice Wiles, now Regius Professor of Divinity at Oxford, writes:

I first knew Ian Ramsey when I went up as an undergraduate immediately after the war. It was a time when entertaining was not easy for dons and in Christ's not over-practised. Ian stood out. His availability to all was well known and welcomed. He also showed his interest in a countless variety of college societies, not only by general benevolence but by his presence at many of their functions, with what even then seemed to me a lavish generosity of time. There was a flourishing college debating society to which he often came and not infrequently spoke, usually finding some reason for speaking from the middle rather than either side of the house. But even the table-tennis club was not too small to attract his presence, and I remember one annual general meeting greatly prolonged by his determination to find just the right procedure on some comparatively trivial matter.

The specifically Christian community, which had a fairly strong evangelistic character in those immediate post-war years, always looked on him as an understanding friend, ready to help in all sorts of ways; but he always let the undergraduate body find its own ethos and never imposed his own. His sermons, preached from notes placed on top of a huge pile of vast prayer books balanced precariously on the altar rail, made an impact—even when (as in, I think, Michaelmas 1945) they constituted a series on Origen, Arius, Athanasius, Locke, Berkeley, and Hume. Our attitude to 'little Ian' was sometimes a little patronising. We knew such a lot in those days! But it was always and without qualification affectionate.

Many similar memories of Ian Ramsey as a pastor survive, together with many careful notes used when introducing undergraduate discussions. He sponsored these discussions in college indefatigably, in addition to the more formal supervisions which he gave in theology and philosophy. There can be little doubt that Christ's College, for all its tensions, was to him a stimulating and rewarding community. And in the background was a history which inspired him. Smuts, the man of action and philosopher of 'holism', was a Christ's man, installed as Chancellor of the University by Raven as Vice-Chancellor in 1948. That year was also the quincentenary of the foundation of the college. In his memoir of Raven, Ramsey recalled how 'on one of the evenings, turning to portraits behind High Table, he pointed to Milton and Darwin as representing two cosmic perspectives which the metaphysics of William Paley, well intentioned, well informed, and clearly argued though it be, could never contain, but which, he believed, might well be harmonised by rehabilitating in our own day some of the distinctive ideas and themes of Ralph Cudworth, the Cambridge Platonist.'

Ramsey, as a scientist and philosopher, was in the habit of taking a pinch of salt with such oratory. In a review, he once wrote: 'Even the most modest philosopher might feel acute embarrassment at being associated with some of the names Dr. Raven mentions—names of those who indulge in reflective generalizations as an innocent hobby.' But this sense that the difficulties in the project were greater than Raven confessed only spurred him on in the attempt to reconcile religion and science. He came to see that the virtue chiefly needed was humility. As he told the British Association in a sermon in Durham Cathedral in 1970: 'The main mistake was to suppose that theology is prescriptive, dictating the answers to which scientific inquiry must come. But the distinctive function of theology is ... to witness to "depth", ... to take seriously the moral dimension.... Theology needs to do a task which it avoided doing for some three hundred years; and deliberately refused to do a hundred years ago. But the road to such an integration, the road to a contemporary mapping or projection of theology, is the same as the road to a scientific culture—though the crucible of contemporary social and moral problems shared by all disciplines.'

But meanwhile, in Cambridge University in the 1940s, there was fulfilment through lecturing and teaching. Much of the fulfilment came because (as H. H. Farmer recalls) his colleagues 're-spected Ramsey's spirit as well as his intellect'; and because he won so many students' hearts. One who went to his lectures remembers how just before Christmas 1946 a large envelope arrived containing 39 foolscap pages of stencilled lecture notes from Ramsey—a service to students which he could imagine coming from no other lecturer at the time. Another, Mary Leeson, writes:

I met Ian during my first term at Girton just over twenty-five years ago. I used to cycle to his house in Hills Road when I felt in need of some family life. I remember how patient Ian was popping spoonfuls into his son Paul's mouth. I also remember Ian's lectures and his amusing, and very helpful, illustrations. He was the only philosopher I could really follow!

3

A Philosophy of 'And More'

DAVID Hume put the challenge in 1748. 'When we run over libraries ... what havoc must we make? If we take in one hand any volume—of divinity or school metaphysics, for instance—let us ask, *Does it contain any abstract reasoning concerning quantity or number?* No. *Does it contain any experimental reasoning concerning matter of fact or existence?* No. Commit it then to the flames, for it can contain nothing but sophistry and illusion.'

Two hundred years later, this challenge was at its height. The emphasis on mathematics and on the 'experimental reasoning' of science resulted in an insistence on the empirical and in a contempt for metaphysics and theology. As Ian Ramsey said at the outset of his *Religious Language*, religion's 'characteristic claim is that there are situations which are spatio-temporal and more'. But he knew how many of his fellow-philosophers regarded the 'more' as nonsense. He introduced his *Christian Discourse* (1965) by saying that he was very conscious of two complaints. 'The one complaint is that contemporary philosophy is a soul-destroying verbalism. The other complaint—rarely made by the same people—is that theology is vacuous chatter, a hollow sham, a bogus pretence, a jungle through which no logical paths may be mapped.' He knew also how widespread was the belief that anything 'more' than the spatio-temporal must be occult. He concluded his *Freedom and Immortality* (1960) with 'a protest against two popular misconceptions: that those with an intense affection for ordinary language must necessarily deny metaphysics, or that those who defend metaphysics must necessarily trade in occult and shadowy worlds. Which means that the book has been fighting on two battle-fronts at once; and it is a sobering reflection that not many wars have been won under such a necessity.'

It seems to be the opinion of all but one or two professional philosophers acquainted with his work that Ramsey did not win: he did not bring to triumph the immensely difficult intellectual task of restating metaphysics and theology in an age of empiricism. But his professional colleagues who knew him all liked him as a man, and almost all of them respected the courage, energy, and ingenuity with which he worked. His philosophy may be judged a brave failure, but in the intellectual situation of the twentieth century this is not usually felt to reflect any discredit on the man. The importance of his task is widely granted—for the rift between logic and mysticism is acknowledged by many to be a cleavage damaging the whole of modern Western civilization—but no one can be pointed to as fully successful in it. Certainly he was more successful than some who have criticized his inadequacies.

When Ramsey began lecturing in Cambridge, he did accept the challenge of those great modern Cambridge figures, G. E. Moore and Ludwig Wittgenstein, to think more clearly. But he could also be humorous about the way in which Moore would spend his Wednesday lecture correcting what he had said on Monday; and about the eccentric Wittgenstein's seance-like classes. In his own lectures he expounded with gusto the metaphysical teachers of the past, specially Bishop Berkeley. He conveyed the impression that many of their teachings could be, and deserved to be, developed without any very radical revision, despite Moore and Wittgenstein. His hearers assumed that it was his own ambition to build a metaphysical system.

Professor Peter Baelz has preserved notes about some of Ramsey's lectures in 1946, and they show an attempt to work towards a philosophical theology, broadly on the lines of a personalist Idealism, but owing a good deal to the tougher kinds of philosophy since the older Idealists. Ramsey presented the world as persons in relation, and persons as centres of experience, their experience being a matter of volition as much as of thought and perception, and their existence and the continuity of their experience being dependent on God as the supreme personal will. The main lines of all this are Berkeleian. Our sensory experience is a medium through which we can become aware of the activity of the divine mind-will. 'Religious experience is unhelpful unless we bring to it a philosophical theology based on sense-experience and value appreciation.'

But the metaphysical system which seemed to be emerging in the 1940s never appeared. One reason was that Ramsey came to see more and more sharply how much in the old metaphysics could not be reconciled with the intellectual integrity of a science-based and analytically clear thinker. Almost the whole subject seemed to need rethinking; and before this could be done, a humbler task had to be accepted. It was necessary to show where and how empiricism was inadequate; where and how metaphysics was more than nonsense.

For example, he accepted the force of the onslaught of C. D. Broad's inaugural lecture at Cambridge in 1934 against the attempt to base the freedom of the will on the idea of a 'timeless self' acting. With other empiricists he questioned whether such an idea is 'even intelligible, let alone true or false'.[1] In his collection of extracts for use by students, *Words about God* (1971), he included key passages from Sir Alfred Ayer's *Language, Truth, and Logic* (1936), including this comment on 'a remark taken at random' from F. H. Bradley's *Appearance and Reality* (1893). The remark was: 'the Absolute enters into, but is itself incapable of, evolution and progress'. The comment was: 'such a metaphysical pseudo-proposition is not even in principle verifiable. For one cannot conceive of an observation which would enable one to determine whether the Absolute did, or did not, enter into evolution and progress.' A comment by Ramsey himself in *Words about God* may be cited (as many similar passages could be) to show that his analysis of the old metaphysics, whether Greek or Victorian, became radical. 'A good deal of the doctrinal controversy of the early church might have been avoided had the Christological problem, for example, been seen to be one of how to use language reliably about Jesus Christ, rather than supposed to be a problem of anthropology or psychology or ontology which asked how two "natures" could be combined into something which, while being completely both, yet was a single homogeneous unity. To phrase the problem in this way is virtually to preclude any intelligible solution.'

Having acknowledged that much validity in the challenge of David Hume and his twentieth-century successors, and having

[1] *Freedom and Immortality*, p. 20.

abandoned his own attempt to build a metaphysical system, Ramsey did, however, believe that the possibility of doing metaphysics could and should be defended. He believed that Kant, for example, or Spinoza before him had been talking something more than 'sophistry and illusion'; and he tried to argue that metaphysics had a future.

In his contribution to a gathering of philosophers at Easter 1959 in Downside Abbey, later published in *Prospect for Metaphysics* (1961), he developed Broad's description of metaphysics as 'critical common sense', for he came to see this branch of philosophy was only strong in so far as it was 'concerned to organize common-sense assertions in accordance with some perspective or other'. So conceived, metaphysics could never deny the observations and experiments of science or common sense. Nor should metaphysical realities be described as if they were physical objects. Indeed, he recalled the famous phrase of Joseph Butler: 'Everything is what it is, and not another thing.' But he commented (p. 159): 'When someone, and it is most often a metaphysician, says X is *really* Y, he need not be denying that X is X. What he is doing by this remark is rather to commend to us his own option for a large-scale map dominated by Y, as that which not only gives a suitable place to talk about X but also, he would claim, gives the best and most illuminating view of the universe.'

So he still insisted on adding Y to X—although he was now equally emphatic that the metaphysical Y differed from the empirical X, for 'metaphysics is no mere extension of ordinary language'. Again and again he spoke of metaphysics as being empiricism 'and more'. Here he did not feel isolated, for he welcomed what he would call the 'broadening' of empiricism among many English philosophers in his lifetime, notably the emphasis on the variegation and richness of languages in the later Wittgenstein, with his slogan: 'Don't look for meanings, look for uses'.

He was particularly interested in the advances made by four brilliant men who became his colleagues in Oxford: Stuart Hampshire,[1] J. L. Austin, P. F. Strawson, and R. M. Hare. He hailed the work of such men as proving how superficial and restricted a view of meaningful language had been embodied in the iconoclastic Verification Principle popularized by the youthful Ayer; and as proving, too, how superficial a view of human personality had been

[1] Notably in his *Spinoza* (1951) and *Thought and Action* (1959).

involved in the attempts to reduce the person in action to the behaviour of a machine. Such men as Hampshire, Austin, Strawson,
and Hare seemed to Ramsey to have opened a more exciting and
productive era in the history of English philosophy. He offered a
study of J. L. Austin in a contribution to an American symposium,[1]
and in a paper on 'Facts and Disclosures' which he read to the
Aristotelian Society in London on 24 January 1972. He compared
Austin in the former paper with Michael Polanyi, in the latter with
P. F. Strawson, whose book *Individuals: An Essay in Descriptive
Metaphysics* (1959) he took very seriously indeed. But he felt specially close to R. M. Hare, the ablest moral philosopher of his generation and a friend who was willing to serve in groups convened by
the Church of England.

Some territory was won back for a 'descriptive' (as contrasted with
'speculative') metaphysics by the work of such 'broadened' empiricists. Ramsey was, however, still convinced that yet further
territory had to be explored, because of his belief that personal
existence—'the Volitional Unity' of his prize essay in 1938, 'the I'
as he now preferred to say—was more mysterious than even the
'broadened' empiricists allowed. He believed, too, that meaningful
language about the person in action could be both straightforwardly
'descriptive' and evocatively more. (That was one reason why he
was so interested in J. L. Austin's category of 'performative' utterances—for example, 'I baptize thee'—as being more than descriptive.) Some of the arguments or illustrations which he used were
of a kind that might have appeared in his Oxford colleagues' books,
possibly with a more professional finish. But for some of the time
when he spoke of 'the I' as an 'integrator' word, and when he
defended metaphysical language about 'the I', he seemed to be
appealing to his own vision of personality (and to his own right
to try to evoke that vision in others) rather than to the common
sense over which his fellow-philosophers preferred to ruminate in
a more even tone of voice. In these passages Ramsey was closer
to the tradition of Kierkegaard, and to the German and French
existentialists of his own day, although (in this, a typically English
philosopher) he made little reference to the Continentals.

In his contribution to the symposium on *Science and Personality*,
he summed up his own philosophy as well as three years of discussion in that group. He had learned from the pioneers of modern

[1] *Intellect and Hope*, ed. T. A. Langford and W. H. Poteat (1968).

philosophical psychology, James Ward and his pupil G. F. Stout, to reject the dualism of mind and body, and to think instead of the embodied self. He recognized the intimate union of the mental or spiritual and the physical, so abundantly demonstrated by modern medicine where, for example, either organic or psychological treatment can be partially effective in psychosomatic illness, or where a drug or an operation on the brain can alter the whole character. But he did believe that there was in some sense a citadel of the 'I', making a personality personal. So to speak, it was a walking citadel. He wrote:

Personally defined in this way would relate to a capacity to meet actively and thus to overcome external forces.... There is no kind of underlying cushion to which all our bodily and mental events and characteristics are attached as pins; and any basic personality matrix is not static. Rather is personality to be enlarged in terms of a distinctive activity, distinctive in being owned, localised, personalised. The unity of personality on this view is to be found in an integrating activity, an activity expressed, embodied and scientifically understood in terms of its genetic, biochemical and endocrine, electronic, neurological and psychological manifestations. What we call human behaviour is an expression of that effective, integrating activity which is peculiarly and distinctly ourselves.

So much might be regarded as the common sense of present-day science. But to Ramsey 'the I' was transcendent in the sense that it was not to be contained within scientific discourse, nor reduced to terms within such discourse. This emphasis on the transcendent 'I' ran through much of his teaching, but he never put it more sharply than in this paper in *Science and Personality*.

Let us argue by a *reductio ad absurdum*. Suppose nothing more were to be said about human beings. Then each human being would be a set—admittedly very complex— of discriminated observables, scientific objects, discerned behaviour patterns, a set of these and no more. This may seem not at all implausible about everybody—except ourselves. As an account by ourselves of ourselves it would clearly be a logical blunder. For any of us to talk of a group of *objects* presupposes a correlative *subject*. Whatever is observed implies an observer who is a presupposition of the resultant discourse and cannot be netted within it.

And he put the same point in a slightly different way in a lecture to a meeting of doctors and theologians at Tübingen in 1967.[1] All

[1] A simplified version was included in *Medicine, Morals, and Man*, ed. E. Claxton (1969).

the scientific disciplines, he said, 'are expressed in the language of observables.... The crucial question then becomes: Can the observer himself be adequately talked of in the language of what he observes?'

Inevitably, the distinction between the observer and the observables (or as it has often been put, between the 'subjective' and the 'objective') has occupied an enormous amount of philosophical attention. Some such distinction was granted in, for example, Gilbert Ryle's *The Concept of Mind* (1949). But Ramsey went much further than Ryle. He put it in his Tübingen lecture in this way. 'Gilbert Ryle like all of us would of course agree that there is a difference between "He has toothache" and "I have toothache"; he would agree that there is more in the second assertion than in the first. But he would say that it is only more in the sense in which "Tommy's doctor uncle" says more than "Tommy's uncle" says.... This kind of more means more observables...' To Ramsey, 'Ryle's approach has reduced the observer to what he is observing.... We have lost the "I" which will always elude capture in the scientific net.'

Why was Ramsey so sure that Professor Ryle—for long more dominant than any other teacher, let alone any other philosopher, in Oxford—was at this point inadequate? At Tübingen he quoted Ryle's argument to the effect that 'the self-elusiveness of "I" is only the elusiveness in today's diary entry which cannot be made until today is past, but which can then be made without any kind of problem or dilemma'. He used another illustration to put his own position. 'Suppose I am struggling to tie a knot and fumbling in the process. I say to myself "I *am* butter fingered". If I were good-tempered I might then laugh out and say "I am laughing at myself for being butter fingered".' To Ramsey, the 'I' was the one who did the condemning or the laughing at the observable behaviour-pattern. So even a diary entry at any depth about 'I' would be more mysterious than Ryle allowed.

But this illustration did not get to the heart of Ramsey's disagreement with Ryle. Nor did his article on 'The Systematic Elusiveness of "I"' in the *Philosophical Quarterly* (1955) for there, as a junior colleague in Oxford, he felt inhibited in criticizing Ryle. All he asked was this: 'May it not be the case that the awareness ... may yet in some way or other be the awareness of some invariant for which "I" with an odd enough logical status could be proper currency? Is there indeed in self-awareness some area which is observationally elusive?' But he hastened to cover himself. 'I am *not* pleading for a self which inhabits an altogether distinct world ... a permanent self untouched by the vagaries of space and time but, if such, also untouched by meanings and arguments alike. So I am quite ready to grant that to date my recommendation is disgustingly small and negative.'

This was indeed a modest self-justification in comparison with Ramsey's inaugural lecture as an Oxford professor (on *Miracles: An Exercise in Logical Mapwork*, 1952), about which Professor Ryle had been heard to express a courteous scepticism. There, he had nailed his colours more firmly to the mast. 'My suggestion is that for each of us "I" is one of our key metaphysical words.... The justification for "I" in particular, and for metaphysical words in general, is given in a non-inferential awareness more concrete than cognition'. And Ramsey never abandoned the metaphysical 'I'—or the metaphysical 'God'. It was his claim that although 'no description is guaranteed', yet 'we might perhaps say that we are as certain of God as we are of ourselves.... God is guaranteed to us very much as we are to ourselves.'[1] But frequent protests from fellow-philosophers brought home to him the general lack of such certainty.

One controversy was with Professor Antony Flew in the *Hibbert Journal* in 1956, under the question 'Can a man witness his own funeral?' Ramsey summed up Flew as saying: 'After death *we* no longer walk, talk, joke, climb mountains or become buried under snow. All that remains is the body.... We may be more than bodies, but what we are *more* perishes at death.' The crux of Ramsey's reply was to assert that personal behaviour was more than Flew had described. The 'I' was 'more than the biological man, the social man, the economic man, the psychological man'. 'Ramsey's funeral', he wrote, 'does not cover all that of which Ramsey is aware when he is aware of myself. It is this *more* for which, on the day of my funeral, philosophical friends, if they feel so inclined, can spend their time choosing logically appropriate phrases. I for my part will be content to enjoy "it" untouched then (I hope) by the need to give it a logical mapping.'

In other words, Ramsey appealed to his own self-awareness, and the appeal was to him the gateway to metaphysics and religion.

[1] *Prospect for Metaphysics*, p. 176.

He told Flew: 'To talk of free will has been to claim that here was something not reducible to predictability stories, causal stories, or any other of the technical tales which would profess to reduce ... a "person" to "objects"—spatio-temporal events.'

When discussing the 'systematic elusiveness of "I"', Ramsey even attempted to teach a lesson in philosophy to David Hume. Hume, he recalled, had rightly said that 'when I enter most intimately upon myself, I always stumble on some particular perception or other, of heat or cold, light or shade, love or hatred, pain or pleasure.' Yet Hume had also confessed to being puzzled by his feeling of personal identity as he reflected on the train of past perceptions that composed a mind. And Ramsey believed that Hume's puzzle should have led him to see that 'persons are in part "invisible and elusive", in part mysterious'—as is disclosed not so much by the memory as by the moral sense. Ramsey grounded metaphysics in ethics because to him what was most self-disclosing was not walking, talking, joking, or climbing, pain or pleasure— but responding to a moral claim. A moral action disclosed the 'and more' that was not dreamed of in Hume's philosophy. For in that response, 'the I' knew what it was to be personal, free, and more than spatial or temporal.

Ramsey had a sophisticated awareness of the problems involved in the emphasis on ethical intuition when it was more usual to regard all moralities, differing greatly between themselves, as the products of indoctrination by families and societies. He knew also that the emphasis on personality, freedom, and immortality needed to be defended when so many of the observations of science seemed to point another way. To demonstrate that he was not a babe in these relativist and reductionist woods, it is enough to point to the one and a half thousand pages of the five symposia which he edited between 1961 and 1971: *Prospect for Metaphysics, Biology and Personality, Christian Ethics and Contemporary Philosophy, Science and Personality*, and *Words about God*. He was also joint-editor of the 'Library of Philosophy and Theology', a major series published by the SCM Press. In those books eminent scientists and philosophers were gathered for a massive and uninhibited debate about the human condition. But while he was familiar with the woods of contemporary discussion, Ramsey kept his own eyes on a single tree.

The conviction from which he never deviated once he had made it his own was expressed in a contribution to the *Cambridge Review* in 1956. This article was a response to R. B. Braithwaite's Eddington Memorial Lecture on 'An Empiricist's View of the Nature of Religious Belief'.[1] Professor Braithwaite had argued that the 'primary use' of Christian assertions was 'to announce allegiance to a set of moral principles' and in particular to declare the Christian's commitment to an 'agapeistic' or loving way of life, connected with 'stories' which encouraged such behaviour. These stories, Braithwaite had suggested, consist of empirical propositions, but the believer who derives moral encouragement from their telling 'need not believe that the empirical propositions presented by the stories correspond to empirical fact'.

To Ramsey, such an interpretation of religious belief was not an adequate account of the believer's response to the moral imperatives of God. For him, this response came before any commitment, and the response to God's claim was a response to fact. In this 1956 article a number of Ramseyan expressions which became familiar, possibly over-familiar, were introduced to the public.

What we have to do to discover *agape* [love], and what I Cor. 13 intends, is to tell a story which begins with a model situation of 'bearing', 'believing', 'hoping' or 'enduring'. Thereafter, this situation is developed in the way that such a qualifying phrase as 'all things' suggests: in other words, we start on an infinite development to which there is no necessary end. The story must be able to go on for ever. With what hope, then, do we pursue and develop it? Until somehow or other a characteristically different situation is evoked, when the light dawns, the penny drops. We pursue the story until in Bradley's sense we are 'satisfied'. At that point *agape* is disclosed, and we respond with an agapeistic way of life....

True, the Christian would say, once the light dawned, 'Love so amazing, so divine, demands my soul, my life, my all'—and he would call this *agape* commitment; but if he did, he would be claiming that I Cor. 13 is fulfilled in what is evoked by the gospel narratives.... When the Christian asserts, 'God is love', he declares *primarily not* his commitment to *agape* or an agapeistic way of life, but his commitment to certain 'facts' somehow or other described in the gospels: 'When I survey the wondrous cross'.

Braithwaite complained in his reply that 'Professor Ramsey

[1] Reprinted, with Ramsey's response, in *Christian Ethics and Contemporary Philosophy*, pp. 53-73, 84-8.

sometimes uses the words "empirical" and "fact" in contexts which surprise (I would almost say shock) me.... Use of these expressions makes it look as if Ramsey were committing the gravest of all category mistakes—that of supposing that an *ought* can follow from an *is*. How can one commit oneself to an empirical fact? How can a fact have a claim on one? ... I suspect that the inverted commas which Ramsey sometimes put round his *facts* indicate that these can only be referred to by statements whose "logic" is "odd" in that it includes the use of special "logical qualifiers". But what is this odd logic? ... How would Professor Ramsey set about teaching this "logic" (or these "logics") to a non-Christian?'

Braithwaite had put his finger on Ramsey's weakness as a philosopher, by complaining that Ramsey could not explain the 'facts' of Christian belief fully to the non-Christian. In part, this was due to Ramsey's own conviction. Although all men had a moral sense which went beyond the biological drive to survival, yet this did not amount to the universal recognition of a Natural Law, let alone God, by the conscience. For Ramsey, there was a disclosure which Christians, and only they, saw. On the other hand, Ramsey had put his hand straight through Braithwaite's reductionist interpretation of religious belief, by indicating more clearly what it feels like to be a Christian responding to the moral claim of God. And he stoutly maintained that there is something similar to this religious response in all morality. As he wrote in a careful essay on 'Moral Judgments and God's Commands' reprinted in *Christian Ethics and Contemporary Philosophy*, the stories told in Christianity do not only encourage the Christian's behaviour: 'they make that behaviour possible'. And he added: 'When in speaking of an action as "good" we commit ourselves to it, are we not recognising a prior claim which that action makes on us? Isn't a commitment always a response to something which is discerned? ... Now such a claim disclosed through and around plain facts has been traditionally spoken of by terms like "Duty" or the "Moral Law" and a theological interpretation arises as and when such terms are theologically contextualised.'

Writing in *Theology* eight years after the publication of his *Religious Language*, Ramsey recalled that its purpose in 1957 had been to defend the objectivity of that to which the Christian responded. '*Religious Language* was written at a time when, to meet attacks on the Christian faith, it was necessary to show (a) that religious language should not be read as if it was flat and altogether descriptive like "Blue copper sulphate turns white on heating" and (b) that "what there is" is not restricted to empirical facts supposed —implicitly if not always explicitly—to be solid, independent, utterly objective sense-data.' He noted: 'Even pink rats have *some* objectivity, some objective reference. . . . This objectivity happens, however, to be more reliably talked of in terms of (say) the excess of alcohol in the digestive system rather than in terms of animals who eat corn and get chased by fox terriers. . . . The claim for objectivity in relation to cosmic disclosures stands or falls on the reliability of what those disclosures enable us to say about God.'

In *Freedom and Immortality* Ramsey tried to present something of what 'cosmic disclosures' disclosed. He introduced this book by referring to Kant's *Critique of Pure Reason*. 'Though neither "God" nor "freedom" nor "immortality", said Kant in effect, could ever be words native to scientific discourse, yet if we consider what is involved in responding to the claims of duty, then we begin to see how to use language about God or freedom or immortality, and the kind of justification which such language can be given. Though I shall say little more about Kant, I am bold to think that his broad claim was reliable. What I hope to show is that these two topics of freedom and immortality are properly united because each makes a similar sort of claim about the universe; because each appeals to a similar kind of situation, a situation not restricted to the "observables" of sense-experience.'

About human freedom, Ramsey said essentially this. 'We make a "free" decision when we are not just this or that behaviour pattern, but when we are "men", when each of us is distinctively "I". At such moments of decision, when all of us characteristically use of ourselves the word "I", this word covers more than all language about objects or all scientific language talks about. The wink on the Promenade at New Brighton differs significantly from a fall of the lid to clean the eye, though this in part it is' (p. 26). 'A free decision is not just a reaction to stimuli but involves all that and something more besides, something which makes it all the more appropriate to speak of it as a response to a challenge, a challenge which is the challenge of "objects" and more' (p. 61).

About immortality, he claimed that 'we are immortal in so far as we know a situation which transcends space and time' (p. 89), but that 'just as with every conviction of freedom there goes an awareness of some obligation, just as freedom is a response to obligation, so with our conviction about our own immortality, there goes an awareness of some Other which—like ourselves—is not restricted to the spatio-temporal' (p. 99). 'Everyone, Christian or not, can reasonably believe in "immortality" ' (p. 143); 'we can mutter with Spinoza. . . . "we discern and discover that we are eternal" ' (p. 83). But it was through Christian worship that the disclosure came most powerfully, leading to this conclusion: 'to the "all-powerfulness" of God, as to the obligations of Duty, we respond "freely". Our response has our personal backing. In both cases we are never more "ourselves" than we are then' (p. 59).

A Christian philosopher, H. D. Lewis who was a close friend, complained in the *Hibbert Journal* (1961) that Ramsey was not definite enough about eternal life. 'He does not quite lose his foothold at any stage,' Professor Lewis wrote, 'but it must also be admitted that he does give his readers some exceedingly anxious moments by leaning so far over on the side of the abyss of silence.' He also complained about the argument for immortality from self-awareness in mortality. 'We may be said in some senses to transcend time, in memory for instance and in anticipation of the future. But there seems to be nothing here peculiar to important decisions or ethical choice', so that Ramsey 'clearly finds a more direct path from certain peculiar situations, such as being confronted by a duty, than I am able to tread'. Ramsey might be in danger of asserting that 'I must have a soul because I am sometimes soulful'. To Lewis, the argument for immortality must rest on its two traditional foundations—the transcendence of the soul (language about the soul as 'a shadowy existent, some kind of counterpart of this body' is 'not altogether bogus') and the transcendence of the God who had revealed his will to hold souls in eternal life. 'It would not be inconsistent to hold a firmly non-physical and substantive view of the self and yet wonder whether this self persists without the body, any more than it would be inconsistent to believe in God without believing that it is his purpose that we should be immortal—the Hebrews at some stage apparently did so.'

Ramsey's reply did little more than to repeat that although immortality must be more than survival 'in terms of plain "going on" ', and although Reinhold Niebuhr was right to declare it 'unwise for Christians to claim any knowledge of either the furniture of heaven or the temperature of hell', yet 'to talk of "I" beginning or

"I" ending is (I would say) just not sense'. As a reply, it was less than satisfactory. For one thing, it seemed to claim that anyone talking sense must assert that every 'I' had existed before the conception of the body or the creation of the world. But we may conclude that what Ramsey really meant was that his own belief in posthumous immortality arose out of his own religious experience.

It was a strongly theistic experience—as critics such as Ninian Smart complained, pointing out that a book entitled *Religious Language* ought to have considered non-theistic religions such as Theravada Buddhism. To Ramsey, God was the 'I' disclosed by all space, by 'the bodily behaviour of the universe'. Sometimes he spoke of religion as consisting of a 'total commitment to the whole universe', and he distinguished this from a captain's commitment to his ship or from a lover's devotion to his beloved (although he went far in claiming that these lesser loyalties were introductions to the greater and quoted the phrase 'You're the whole world to me'). In a paper given to the Modern Churchmen's Union in 1964,[1] he wrote: 'It may be that we are walking in remote, mountainous country, and as night comes on we are filled with all kinds of uncertainties and anxieties. But then we refresh ourselves at a mountain stream, look up to the stars as symbols of stability, and find our path illuminated by the moon. A sense of kinship with nature strikes us; the universe is reliable after all.'

In the best treatment of 'Ian Ramsey on Talk about God' which has so far appeared (in *Religious Studies*, June and September 1971), Professor Donald Evans points out how personal this view of the universe was. 'Whether or not the universe seems friendly rather than hostile or neutral or conflictual depends a great deal on the individual's conscious and unconscious view of himself and of other human beings. Indeed, whether or not he sees a universe at all—as Ramsey does—rather than an unintegrated multiverse or even a chaos, depends to a great deal on the extent to which his own personality is well-integrated. World-views and depth psychology are intimately related.'

The passage just quoted from Ramsey, about kinship with nature, is justly called by Evans 'Wordsworthian'. As the product of a scientific and urban environment, however, Ramsey did not concentrate on the beauty of nature. Indeed, as a post-Darwinian man he often alluded to nature's apparent ruthlessness. Rather,

[1] *Reprinted in Myth and Symbol, ed. F. W. Dillistone (1966).*

God was for him the supreme fact which 'integrated' all scientific talk about observables and his lectures on *Religion and Science* had this as their central theme, suggesting some kinship between this function of 'God' (in what he elsewhere called 'an over-all language map') and scientific invariants such as points, force, mass, and so forth, around which the observables can be organized. But even more powerfully, God was disclosed in the model of personality; for to Ramsey, the personal was always supreme. Indeed, in *Religion and Science* he claimed that science itself is based on the scientist's intuitive sensitivity to the universe and to the rational pattern in its disclosures. He also claimed that science uses 'symbols or expressions that echo personal disclosures' (such as 'harmony' or 'opposition'). In the third of his lectures on *Christian Discourse*, he spoke of the model of God as 'a Whole', and showed that it arose out of the use of the idea of God in integrating everything. But he made clear his own preference for the model of God as 'a Person'. He said: 'Disclosures reveal objectivity. It is certainly not the "objectivity" which belongs to physical objects and ... to other "people" as topics of social statistics. *It is the objectivity of what declares itself to us*—and challenges us in a way that *persons may do*' (p. 88).

In a private paper, 'A Personal Credo', which he prepared for the Church of England's doctrinal commission in 1972, Ramsey showed that he was still thinking about the criticisms made of his claims that 'disclosure' showed something or someone 'objective' and transcending the universe.

In the first place, he said, 'we are originally relatively passive' until 'we are confronted by something other than ourselves, something or someone whose activity bears on our own. It is only then that in response "we come alive", "find ourselves", and actively express our response as commitment. We now need to introduce the term "cosmic disclosure".' In the second place, 'a cosmic disclosure is one from which, in principle, nothing is excluded'. 'With cosmic disclosures there is no good reason to suppose more than one individuation, more than one source of the activity which confronts us on these occasions. There is no reason to suppose more than one reference common to these occasions, than there is to suppose more than one universe. I give the name *God* to the single individuation of which we are actively aware in all cosmic disclosures.' And he added one example of language which makes the point that 'nothing is excluded' from a 'cosmic disclosure'. He referred to the slogan that 'duty is independent of particular consequences', and he interpreted it as meaning not that 'consequences do not matter' but that 'a disclosure of duty is all-compelling, and in this sense has taken account of all possible consequences'.

But what, or who, is God?

The first section of Ramsey's anthology of *Words about God* was a collection of testimonies mainly from the Christian Fathers that the divine mystery is unutterable, and included this warning from the Jewish philosopher, Moses Maimonides: 'I do not merely declare that he who affirms attributes of God has not sufficient knowledge concerning the Creator ... but I say that he unconsciously loses his belief in God'. And his contribution to *Prospect for Theology*,[1] Ramsey showed himself well aware of the difficulties involved in speaking of 'A Personal God'. But he there argued that 'we may attribute "personality" to God if there occur ... cosmic situations of a disclosure kind, whose patterns are isomorphous with disclosures of personal reciprocity. When this reciprocity is such as characterises situations of kindness and loving concern, we then have situations which justify talk of grace and prayer and which, at least in that kind of context, might also justify talk of miracles and providence.... When the universe comes alive in a cosmic disclosure where structure is modelled by a personal reciprocity, it declares itself to us as a person does; and as a characterization of the activity which we then know, "person" is the most natural model of any to use.'

In his paper to the Modern Churchmen's Union already cited, Ramsey listed the many models used to talk about God in the Old Testament—including the image of God as a dairymaid (Job 10:10) or metal worker (Mal. 3:3). He showed that this use of many models in religion has an analogy in ordinary language and in science, when models are used to talk about X. 'Any one model would enable us to be articulate about X in some way or another, but if we wanted to talk as adequately as possible about X we should build out the most consistent, comprehensive, coherent, and simple discourse from as many models as possible. Now, if we did this, my contention is that we should see a language emerging which fitted closer to the language which a believer uses about God.'

[1] A symposium in honour of H. H. Farmer, ed. F. G. Healey (1969).

How, then, should models be used in speaking about God? In his second lecture on *Religious Language*, Ramsey showed how by adding 'qualifiers' to models believers attempted to safeguard the wonder of the divine mystery. Some of these 'qualifiers' are negative. Thus the philosophical phrase 'immutable' safeguards the insight that, however active God is, he is also to be spoken of as unchanging (in terms of the hymn 'Abide with me'), so that 'if anything is mutable it will not be exact currency for God'. Other 'qualifiers' are used more positively to suggest the transcendent unity, simplicity, and perfection of God. Thus to say that God is 'the *first* cause' is to say that he is 'logically prior to all causal stories'; and to say that God is '*infinitely* wise' or '*infinitely* good' is much more than to say that he is very, very clever or very, very moral.

Ramsey used this approach to reduce the severity of a problem notoriously involved in talk about God as good. How can God be good if he sentences most, or any, of his children to 'everlasting' punishment?

This problem had caused a major controversy around the Victorian theologian F. D. Maurice, and in the first of his Maurice Lectures[1] Ramsey endeavoured to take some of the heat out of hell. He summed up Maurice's message as being that 'we must so talk about eternity, even eternal punishment or eternal death, that the phrases lead to God'. His own teaching was that the qualifier 'eternal' does not mean merely continuing for ever; the point of the word is to draw our minds away from time. And the model of 'punishment' by God must mean this: 'When the loving father punishes (in whatever way he judges best) the sense of opposition and separation, which undoubtedly occurs, nevertheless yields at its climax a kinship of deeper love—a richer reconciliation.'

In his 1969 Presidential Address to the Society for the Study of Theology, Ramsey spoke on 'The Concept of the Eternal'.[2] He claimed that his understanding of 'eternal' as qualifying the religious use of models by no means impoverished the concept. From the history of philosophy he showed how eternity has been understood variously as lasting unendingly, as not conditioned by time, as the Whole which contains all time, as the eminence from

---

[1] Delivered at King's College, London, in 1961, and published as *On Being Sure in Religion* (1963).

[2] Published by the SPCK in a collection on *The Christian Hope* (1970).

which all time is viewed, and as the reality of which time is a moving image. All these partial understandings can, he claimed, be regarded as attempts to interpret the cosmic disclosure in which all talk about eternity is grounded.

In *Models and Mystery* (1964), Ramsey compared the religious use of models with their scientific use as discussed in Max Black's *Models and Metaphors*, and with their functions in the social sciences. Some models, he pointed out, are 'scale' or picturing models—such as a model yacht. Others, no less useful, are 'analogue' or 'disclosure' models, 'guided by the more abstract aim of reproducing the structure of the original'. And some of these latter are characterized by the fact that 'their objective reference is never given independently of the model'.[1] Relating these secular uses of models to the current tasks of a self-critical theology, Ramsey wrote: 'The great virtue of a model is that it enables us to be articulate when before we were tongue-tied. But it is evident that articulation is now much more tentative that it was before, when it was developed on the basis of a scale model.' Certainly 'there must be something about certain cosmic situations which matches those situations in which men find themselves in the presence of a judge or a king' (or a father), yet there can be no exact comparison between earthly rulers and the King of kings, for 'the theological model works more like the fitting of a boot or shoe than like the yes or no of a roll-call'. Ramsey came to call this rough correspondence between the theological model and the empirical facts an 'empirical fit'. But 'in theology, the model must occur in a phrase which incorporates also a qualifier which in its simplest form will be a word or suffix designed to make sure that here the main point of the model is seen to be its fulfilment in a disclosure'.

Inevitably such an interpretation of religious language was questioned by fellow-philosophers, although almost all granted that it did more justice to religious experience and symbolism than was done in the attempt by, for example, R. B. Braithwaite. The crux of the questioning was put by R. W. Hepburn in the periodical *Philosophical Books* (January 1965): 'On what grounds do we say that the development of religious models converges upon an ever more adequate conception of an actual deity? How can we know when such a disclosure is or is not veridical? How do we tell

[1] *Myth and Symbol*, p. 89.

whether our seeming-cosmic disclosure reveals the nature of the whole or just a fragment (an untypical sample perhaps)?' Professor Hepburn's conclusion was that Ramsey had ingeniously given 'a new name to a nest of old problems'.

In a lively paper,[1] Ninian Smart protested that there appeared to be no means of falsifying any cosmic disclosures, or of invalidating the use of any model in religion, on Ramsey's showing. A Buddhist might claim that ultimate was impersonal, or that there was not even an ultimate 'it', on the basis of a 'disclosure', or the Hindu might appeal to the splendid 'disclosure' described in the *Bhagavad Gita*; and Ramsey could not argue back. As for models, it might be asserted that God was a 'sphere' (or as Smart thinks he said in the actual discussion with Ramsey, a 'tomato'), with the qualifier 'perfect'. Smart said firmly: 'An account of religious discourse which appeals to disclosure (or revelation of religious experience, etc.) must indicate why there are (rather radically) different ways of expressing what it is that disclosures disclose. It must give guidance as to what considerations would be relevant in choosing one set of doctrines rather than another.' And Ramsey also seemed unable to answer atheism, for all his talk about the 'I' and 'God' being 'logical kinsmen'. 'Whereas our existence is not in dispute, this is hardly true of God. One still needs to indicate why persons do not have to "come alive", while on Ramsey's account the universe only sometimes does so.'

In *Theology* (January 1965) Professor Smart pressed home the attack—although, as he assured Ramsey at the time, no personal abuse was intended. Religious language, Smart claimed, must somehow *describe* ultimate reality, not merely engineer the discernment of it. 'If we take the descriptions away, we take truth away. That is why Ramsey's position, though it so far need not entail atheism, is compatible with it. . . . God becomes a name for penny-dropping experiences. . . . It is as though someone was to say that God was the name for all patches of blue. . . . Ramsey thus has really dispensed with transcendence. . . . This is equivalent to a superstitious atheism.'

In the journal *Theoria to Theory* (April 1967), three critics made more detailed attacks. R. B. Braithwaite found imprecision in all Ramsey's key terms. His use of 'model', 'discernment', and 'disclosure' was not genuinely paralleled in science. For example, 'when

---

[1] Printed in the 1959 Supplementary Volume of the Aristotelian Society, on *Paradox in Religion*.

the scientist conjectures the hypothesis it is not *disclosed* to him that it is true. Indeed most conjectured hypotheses turn out to be false.' As for the religious commitment to a disclosure, 'the sincere attempt to follow Ramsey's instruction may, as it does for many religiously-minded people, lead to a disclosure not of something in any way "beyond" but of something for which "within" is by far the most appropriate metaphor.'

Joan Miller's criticism fastened on what many philosophers regarded as Ramsey's loose and confusing talk about 'disclosures'. 'I am led to suppose by the absence of any criteria that what is disclosed is how Ramsey feels about a given situation, and whether there is an empirical fit or not is decided by whether it fits his own view of the world.' Ted Bastin added that whereas 'the scientist wants to see his model specifying the facts as precisely as possible, and his ideal is for the practitioners of his science to take to his model so completely that they cease to distinguish between the facts as they are specified by his model and the facts as they really are', Ramsey suggested 'that you are actually exhibiting theism when you skate precariously from one partly baked idea to another and avoid getting tied down to any definition'. Bastin concluded: 'Logically this position is untenable, and practically it is far too like an attempt to make Christianity safe for vague thinking.'

Ramsey replied gently, and at some length, to these criticisms. He told Smart that 'it is more exciting than true to call me an atheist'. He told his *Theoria to Theory* critics that 'what I try to do is to give a logic of theological stammering', knowing that 'theology which is too well cooked is disastrous'. But while he vindicated his own intentions—not least because he added 'a word of gratitude to my friends'—his defences of his philosophical statements did not convince these critics.

On the other hand, John Macquarrie—for example, in his examination of the logic and language of theology, *God-Talk* (1967)—is one of those who have paid tribute to Ramsey's philosophical work. 'The nature of analogical discourse about God has', Macquarrie there wrote, 'perhaps been brought out most clearly among recent writers on theological language by Ian Ramsey, with his terminology of "models" and "qualifiers".' Macquarrie's own stress on the existential element in theology—'that is to say, our first-hand participation in the experiences and situations which theology tries to explicate'—was close to 'the kind of "disclosures" of which

Ramsey talks', and Macquarrie connected Ramsey's position with
John Locke's brand of empiricism, which allowed the experience of
inner sense to stand alongside the data of the senses of sight, hearing, touch, and the rest. (Not for nothing did Ramsey introduce
Locke's *The Reasonableness of Christianity* in a new edition in
1958.) Looking back in 1973 Professor Macquarrie has written:
'Ramsey told me that although his method and vocabulary were
very different from mine, we were in fundamental agreement on
many theological issues, and I am pleased to think that this is true.
I certainly thought of him as the leading exponent in England of
the application of analytic philosophy to theological problems, and
as a Christian thinker he entered into dialogue with the toughest
philosophical school of our time.'

   In *Theology* for February 1971, Professor H. P. Owen congratu-
lated Ramsey on 'an original theory of religious language' and 'a
major and distinctive service to Christian philosophy'. 'Certainly
there is a marked similarity between his theory of models and
qualifiers and the Thomist doctrine of analogy. But he offers a
wholly novel restatement of the doctrine.' Ramsey's entire enterprise was 'animated by a desire to be faithful to both Scripture and
tradition', and his writings contained 'no trace of liberalism in the
bad sense that mars so much Protestant, and by no means least
Anglican, theology. They contain no compromise with the *Zeitgeist*,
no reduction of doctrines to what seems to be immediately accept-
able to "modern man", no sneers at those who, inevitably, employed
thought-forms other than those which modernists represent as being
"relevant" to our condition.' But, while deeply Christian, Ramsey's
teaching was said by Owen to combine the best in both empiricism
and existentialism. 'His theology is empirical in so far as he shows
how our symbols of God have roots in finite experience and are
qualified in ways for which we can produce finite analysis. Equally
his theology is existentialist in so far as he insists that the disclosure
of God occurs through personal situations, and that it demands an
appropriate commitment. At the same time he avoids any tendency
to equate theistic statements with their empirical grounds or to
assume that the latter constitute verification of the former. Also he
avoids the irrationalism and obscurity by which much existentialist
theology is marred.'

   As a way of indicating the inspiration behind his philosophical
work, on many occasions Ramsey retold the story of King David

and the prophet Nathan (II Sam. 12:1-11). David had 'come alive' and had 'come to himself' as the ice had broken and the light had dawned with Nathan's 'You are the man!' He loved to preach about the New Testament's similar stories of men and women meeting Jesus and finding God revealed, as when the friends at the supper table in Emmaus suddenly knew the Easter victory. For such biblical stories fitted into his own religious experience. He was the man; he had seen. 'Here I would say', he wrote in the *Hibbert Journal* (July 1965), 'are situations so universal and unexpected as to be striking—occasions of disclosure. By a logical parallel with situations of free will, such situations ... can then license talk about God's personal activity. For it is around a striking nonconformity that our free, spontaneous, and characteristically personal activity is displayed as distinct from some routine behaviour pattern whose centre is for each of us his body.'

Here another criticism of Ramsey was possible: he never dealt adequately with the historical side of the question whether miracles occurred.[1] 'What I want to know', Professor Flew protested to Ramsey at one philosophical meeting, 'is whether the corpse walked.' Flew was not satisfied with the answer. But Ramsey did not really depend on history. His personal experience of seeing God's self-disclosure, supremely in Jesus Christ, was what enabled him to assure Professor Braithwaite in 1967 that 'on my view, God is other than the universe (let alone the world) as he who discloses himself in and through it, something like, though not exactly like, the way we disclose ourselves through our bodily behaviour.' And Ramsey also made clear that even sacred scriptures or his own favourite phrases were to him mere models, needing qualification and always falling short of the disclosure. Indeed, C. P. Snow, observing him over the years, reached the conclusion that, although Ramsey was for so long professionally engaged in the interpretation of religious language, words did not matter ultimately to him, any more than history did. What could be observed scientifically was best expressed in the mathematical formulae which he had loved as a boy. What mattered more to him was his experience, too deep for words.

---

[1] Although he did contribute on 'History and the Gospels: Some Philosophical Reflections' to *Studia Evangelica*, vol. iii (Berlin, 1964). This was part of the proceedings of an international conference in Oxford.

FOR FURTHER READING

The invaluable articles by Professor Donald Evans are mentioned above (p. 41). Professor Jerry H. Gill kindly allowed me to read his forthcoming book on Ian Ramsey's philosophy in manuscript, although in order not to plagiarize I refrained from taking notes. Dr. Gill also has in preparation a collection of Ian Ramsey's philosophical papers. Dr. Michael Durrant has in preparation a volume of essays by former pupils of Ian Ramsey, developing points in his teaching.

The collections of essays which Ramsey edited (see p. 36) give the background to his work, but more recently published introductions include *Russell* by A. J. Ayer and *Wittgenstein* by David Pears in the 'Fontana Modern Masters' series. Examples of how sympathetic, but non-theological, philosophers now assess the classic metaphysicians are provided by W. H. Walsh, *Metaphysics* (1963), and by the two Peregrine Books (1969) on *Berkeley* by G. J. Warnock, and on *F. H. Bradley* by Richard Wollheim. See also G. J. Warnock, *Contemporary Moral Philosophy* (1967), for a call for a fresh attempt to relate 'ought' to 'is'. An excellent introduction to the use of models, etc., in religion—a richer use than was acknowledged by any of the earlier analysts of 'God-talk'—has been provided by Thomas Fawcett, *The Symbolic Language of Religion* (1970).

4

A Professor and More

THE Oxford years were in many ways the happiest. But Professor Ramsey could not be entirely comfortable; for the Nolloth Professor of the Philosophy of the Christian Religion in the University of Oxford occupies a strange position, with many philosophers believing that the Christian religion cannot be philosophized about and survive. The chair was endowed in order to provide suitable support for C. C. J. Webb, a much respected teacher of the old school. His successor in 1930, L. W. Grensted, was interested mainly in the psychology of religion and in pastoral counselling.[1] On Grensted's retirement in 1950 there was talk of abolishing the chair and it was refused by a number of philosophers, who objected particularly to the regulation confining it to communicant members of the Church of England. When he was first sounded, Ramsey joined this protest and declined to be a candidate, sorely tempted as he was. He accepted election (at the age of thirty-six) only after the chair had been thrown open to all.

Even after striking this little blow for freedom, Ramsey faced many difficulties in justifying his position. The Oxford Honours School of Theology was severely biblical and historical, and few undergraduates chose to take the optional paper in the philosophy of religion. Many of the leaders of Christian thought in Oxford adhered to a more conservative theology than did Ramsey. This was the heyday of C. S. Lewis (already known to Ramsey because

---

[1] Ramsey collected passages from Grensted's writings for a privately printed memoir (1966).

his home was in Headington Quarry parish). Christian belief often seemed to be treated as an inherited tradition, appealing to the imagination, producing holiness and courtesy—but ill at ease both with science and with democracy. The need to develop a dialogue between a traditional theology and the new philosophy was increasingly recognized, but the stress was on being thoroughly professional, and, to be blunt, Oxonian, in philosophy. The key figure in the Christian dons' discussion group known as 'the Metaphysicals', which Ramsey joined, was the brilliantly graceful and ingenious Austin Farrer, who made no secret either of his affection or of his suspicion towards the newcomer. When Basil Mitchell edited a collection of essays by members of this group on *Faith and Logic* (1957), no essay by the Nolloth Professor was included.

Ramsey therefore had to win his way among the Oxford Christians. More challenging still was the philosophical climate, recalled by Lady Helen Oppenheimer:

The philosophical world of Oxford in the early 1950s was a strenuous and exciting world, a curious mixture of the liberating and the circumscribing. One seemed to be let out of a large but stuffy room on to a fresh and enticing but narrow path which one could explore with delight so long as one did not stray into metaphysics.

The door had been opened by Wittgenstein, but at that stage this was still something of a secret door. The *Blue and Brown Books*, the lecture notes which had been the key, were still circulating half under cover in typescript. A more accessible way out had opened in 1949 in the shape of Professor Ryle's *Concept of Mind*. Now one was set free into an outdoor world. People were whole beings not mysterious combinations of body and mind. Worries about the reality of the material world or whether anybody else existed could be put behind one: but at the cost of discovering that there were some ideas which could never be formulated, some things which there was no point in trying to say. Most of one's fellows seemed to pay this price gladly, and philosophers seemed to be characteristically watchdogs against nonsense rather than explorers.

Helen Oppenheimer remembers Ramsey's lectures, which she attended as part of her work for the newly instituted degree of B.Phil.

One appreciates the books more and maybe understands them better for having been at the lectures, for having had to try to make notes on this excitement bordering on incoherence, this terrier-like worrying away at a concept, these repeated approaches to certain basic positions, the enthusiastic diagrams on the blackboard, all directed towards helping the penny to drop and the light to dawn.

One could not call him a superb teacher: he was too 'involved', in more than one sense of the word. Nor is 'prophet' quite the right word. He seemed rather with a most characteristic courtesy and humility to take the role of an inspiring senior colleague, working both ahead of one and beside one in a common enterprise in which his ideas were available almost before he had really sorted them out to encourage and enliven one's own thinking.

Dr. Michael Durrant, one of a considerable number of Ian Ramsey's pupils who later held academic posts in philosophy, recalls the graduate classes at 5.15 on a Thursday evening.

Ian's classes became the stage for many a dramatic scene which called for his talents as a producer and controller to be brought forth in full measure—which they indeed were. Further, he always made some positive contribution to the discussion in which he usually managed to forge a connexion with his own central thesis concerning 'disclosures'. We often felt that these attempts were, to say the least, based on fragile connexions between the points made and hence built on unsure foundations and, to say the most, we sometimes felt that they were far fetched. But I think we always had some admiration for his attempts to make his own theses and positions relevant, since it was a mark of intellectual honesty and involvement that he should do so. To have declined to do so and let the discussion pass by would have been to take the easy way out and Ian was too honest and too committed to his own position to permit this to happen. Indeed he never took the easy way out of anything; he was always prepared to consider the objector's case in its fully fledged form. What stood out about these seminars was the great deal of hard work and preparation that Ian put into them: nothing was slipshod and he never relied upon the particularities of the occasion to be the sole source of his comments and contribution.

One of the American graduates who came to Oxford to study under him was Dr. Jerry Gill, who has this memory of Ramsey at meetings of philosophical societies.

It was characteristic of Ian, both in his writing and in his person, to take up a conciliatory position between two equally forceful but conflicting perspectives. Thus in theology he sought a middle-ground between existentialist and orthodox emphases ('the Resurrection of Christ is certaintly more than an empty tomb, but it is at least that'), while in philosophy he combined a respect for empiricism with a concern for values ('talk of God must be anchored in experiential models which disclose a commitment that is both human and more'). Nowhere was his conciliatory posture more directly evident than in his personal relationships with colleagues of differing points of view. At professional meetings involving both philosophers and theologians, encounters combining British formality with ideological antipathy, Ian was continually building bridges and destroying barriers, both with his insights and with his genuine, personal warmth. Though they could not always agree with him, the likes of Gilbert Ryle and Antony Flew on the one hand and H. D. Lewis and Ninian Smart on the other clearly respected Ian, first as a thinker, but perhaps more as a true human being.

Those glimpses must be enough to disclose Ramsey's teaching methods in Oxford. But it should be added that one ex-pupil, Professor Donald Evans, who says frankly that Ian Ramsey meant as much to him as his own parents did, points to the price paid when he writes: 'I was always more impressed by his ability to discover plans or possibilities in others, than by his own work. I often thought that if he had devoted less time and energy to me and countless others, and more to his own work, it would have been immeasurably better. One of the reasons why I wrote my *Religious Studies* articles about him was that I felt he had not done justice to himself.'

Yet it was his chosen way. It is significant and consoling that Ramsey himself so often taught that 'the I' was best seen through activity. As Helen Oppenheimer recalls his frequent expositions of Bishop Berkeley's philosophy, it is the insistence on the person in action that comes to her mind. She writes:

It is commonly thought that in reducing all 'being' to 'being perceived', to ideas in the mind, Berkeley was inconsistent in stopping short of his own being: that he was simply a forerunner to Hume's more drastic reduction of the human person as well as the material world to a 'congeries of perceptions', minds, like matter, becoming bundles of ideas. To stipulate as Berkeley did that we have no 'ideas' of persons as we have of things but rather 'notions' is assumed to be an expedient, like saying that God is always about in the quad. Ian Ramsey agreed that Berkeley's theory of mind was a matter of undeveloped hints and insights and that he almost delivered himself into Hume's hands: but he suggested that Berkeley was really feeling after and pleading for something more peculiar than an objective 'idea' of a person: for a kind of awareness which each of us has in being active, which can yield a more subtle and significant concept of personality.

To this difficult but rewarding distinction between the active and the inert, the subjective and the objective, usefully indicated in the difference between 'I' and 'me', legitimately signalised by Berkeley's use of the word 'notion', Ian Ramsey constantly recurred in lectures and in print, approaching it from different directions so that the penny should drop, the light dawn, and 'activity' itself should be a disclosure word. Here in the concept of the active person was his link between the public world into which *The Concept of Mind* had opened a way, and the real mysteries which remain when all the dusting and sweeping and dissolving of puzzles has been done. The human being is not a ghost inhabiting a machine, an intellect imprisoned in a body, but *one* and *active*. 'Concepts such as body and mind, body and soul are to be subsumed under the concept of person, that activity which informs our very being that which makes each of us himself or herself.'[1]

Whatever it thought of the merits of Ramsey's philosophy, Oxford could not help noting that he was uncommonly active. As Dr. Henry Chadwick recalls: 'for energy, affection, and human kindness he was one in ten thousand.' His Maurice Lecture on 'Christian Social Duty' rested on his personal practice.[2]

Almost every Oxford don has to undertake duties both as a fellow of his college and as a member of his faculty, but Ramsey discharged his duties with a striking gusto and asked for more. As a Fellow of Oriel, he not only played a full part in the social and chapel life of the college (he had become 'Uncle Ian' to students), but was also more active in college business than was expected of a professor. For two terms, during a vacancy in the Treasurership, he was in charge of the college's estates and investments. He not only served his year as Chairman of the Faculty of Theology, but in 1952 accepted fresh commitments as Faculty Librarian, as a member of the

---

[1] Ian Ramsey in *From Fear to Faith*, ed. Norman Autton (1971), p. 82.
[2] *On Being Sure in Religion*, pp. 26-47.

General Board of the Faculties covering the whole university, and as Treasurer of Ripon Hall (he had been a Governor since 1946).

He was becoming more and more involved in administration. In his Zenos Lectures in 1966,[1] he surprised his Chicago audience by the nature of his discussion of the Holy Spirit, for with an equal zest he emphasized both that the Spirit is 'disclosed' by the 'model' of a gale or typhoon and that the Spirit always makes for order and efficiency. He devoted his second lecture to an examination of the Fathers' use of the word 'economy' as a model for God's providence, God's care of human needs. He denounced any tendency to speak of administration in a pejorative sense. Instead, the lecture ended: 'It might have been said, he who knows economy knows God and economy is what the word God means.'

He was now in the habit of standing up for what he thought was the right course in administration. Some of his Oriel colleagues thought him a bit of a nuisance in his insistence on certain details of college business; while some fellow-theologians thought it most odd that he should be so concerned about the business of the Faculty Board. He certainly could become tiresome. He got into the papers by parking his car outside Oriel and at first refusing to pay the fine because it was unjust. (He argued that a lot of other cars were parked but not punished.) And the building of his house, High Quarry on Harcourt Hill, involved a great dispute. He later told the story to the House of Lords. 'The only way I got a decision about building a house, when my application had reached some kind of joint planning committee the length of whose title was a clear symbol of inefficiency and delay, was by a threat not only to appeal to the Minister but to sit in his Department until a decision was reached.'

But three of his activities call for more serious notice.

In 1964 he became Director of the Lambeth Diploma in Theology, supervising the studies of men and women who had missed out on the opportunity to take a theology degree. His pupils gratefully recall how he sacrificed Saturday mornings to such tuition—and kept the coffee pot hot under a cushion until they arrived.

He joined the Warneford and Park Hospitals Management Committee in 1954, and was Chairman from 1960. Here again he enjoyed battles with higher authorities. 'I got the impression,' he told the Lords, 'that many, if not most, Ministry circulars were designed

---

[1] Published posthumously as *Models of Divine Activity* (1973).

to keep my colleagues and myself from exercising any novel policies whatever.' It is clear, however, that this involvement in the life of a great and expanding hospital for the mentally ill gave Ramsey scope for his energies; and it was thoroughly appropriate that the pastoral staff which he used as a bishop was a gift from his friends in the Warneford. He loved the social functions and the chapel services, and brought much to them. But he also loved and served the whole place, as Dr. R. G. McInnes, Physician-Superintendent, 1938-67, recalls.

My relationship with Professor Ramsey was one of happily increasing friendship throughout the years when we worked so intimately together. He was such a reasonable and warm-hearted man that one could not but feel better for being with him.

For over forty years I walked the wards of psychiatric hospitals with chairmen and members of committees. It is no easy task for people who are relatively unaccustomed to talking with mentally-ill patients to be confronted with them, either singly or in a group, and always to find the right word for the situation. Ramsey had a remarkable gift for this. His sensitivity was such that even in the presence of only the most exiguous signals he could find his way unerringly in the paths of easy communication. Not only so but there was always the likelihood that he would, by a word, a gesture, or an attitude, illuminate afresh a situation which had become ordinary through familiarity and thereby regenerate hope and confidence in the values and beliefs for which he stood.

He was both meticulous and enthusiastic in his administrative work. Meetings of the Hospital Management Committee took place monthly, although there were numerous sub-committee meetings at other times, most of which the chairman attended. It was his custom to arrive at 9 a.m. The next two hours were spent on going through the agenda with me and the Group Secretary. Nothing was too small for consideration if it was of human importance to a patient or member of the staff; or if it was relevant in some way to larger issues affecting the hospital and its future. It was often in these pre-committee sessions that one had the best opportunity to see his acutely analytical mind at work—looking for significances, arranging priorities, foreseeing consequences arising from possible decisions. In the actual meetings of the committee the agenda was usually long; but Ramsey never allowed any member or any item to be hurried. Everyone had a chance to speak and time in which to do it. The chairman spoke a good deal himself and was always in control of the proceedings; yet no one felt overborne, and the almost invariable result of this kind of procedure was the emergence of a con-

sensus of opinion which made voting unnecessary except on very rare
occasions.

The third activity to be mentioned is his heavy involvement in
various groups meeting in London and elsewhere to discuss aspects
of the Church of England's social responsibility. He took all the
more interest in such groups because they specialized in the ethical
problems of medicine. The confusion of current thinking about
religion and medicine was revealed to him by his membership of the
Commission on Divine Healing which met at Archbishop Fisher's
behest between 1954 and 1957. Ramsey would say that this was the
most puzzling exercise he had ever known; he would come home
after each meeting with his mind in a complete whirl. When in
1956 G. R. Dunstan was organizing a group to prepare for the
Church of England a really competent report on birth control and
associated questions, Ramsey was delighted by the opportunity to
bring to bear the clarifying methods of philosophy.

The Report on *The Family in Contemporary Society* (1958) was
probably the ablest document in this field to be produced by
any Christian group. Its conclusions were adopted by the Anglican
bishops in their Lambeth Conference that summer, and were all the
more impressive ten years later in comparison with papal pro-
nouncements. The Anglican document firmly blessed sexual inter-
course as the God-given means of building up marriage, and
marriage as the God-given means of rearing a rationally planned
and limited family. A child should be born out of the free decision
of partners in love. Ramsey was right to reprint the report's theological discussion of contraception—the part of the work where he was
the leader—in his collection on *Christian Ethics and Contemporary
Philosophy*.

The success of this brain-child encouraged Ramsey to play a
major part in later groups which G. R. Dunstan organized on behalf
of the Church of England's Board for Social Responsibility. These
produced the reports *Ought Suicide to be a Crime?* (1959), *Sterilization* (1962), *Punishment* (1963), *Decisions about Life and Death*
(1965), and *Abortion* (1965). In each case the group honestly grap-
pled with an ethical dilemma, partly in connection with the enact-
ment or operation of the law of England; in each case it studied
the evidence thoroughly; and in each case it found that although
no easy answers were possible sufficient agreement about Christian

insights could be reached to justify a conclusion which might for brevity's sake be described as cautiously liberal. Liberal: the first in this series of reports, urging that suicide should be viewed as a tragedy but not as a crime, had influence with the Government in framing the Suicide Act of 1960, as the relevant White Paper acknowledged. But also cautious: the report on sterilization was more hesitant about its use in limiting the population than liberal opinion was tending to be. The report which enjoyed the widest publicity was that on abortion, where the Church of England was seen to be diverging from the Roman Catholic Church's traditional teaching that the sacrifice of a foetus to a mother's health is in no case justified.

These groups heartened Ramsey's conviction that philosophy could illuminate religious and moral problems. They also confirmed his view that in the modern world of many specialisms, many problems could not be tackled except by group-work. The day of the solitary authority was over. Ramsey grew convinced that a decision about abortion (for example) needed a group. So did the running of any part of industry—or of the Church. In his teaching, the importance of groups became as prominent as the importance of disclosures. Indeed, the group was often what had the disclosure.[1]

When in 1966 a new Bishop of Durham was being sought, this contribution to the Church of England's rethinking of its social responsibility was (it seems) what chiefly commended the name of Ian Ramsey. At any rate, it was appropriate that he should spend the night before he went to do homage in Buckingham Palace in the home of G. R. Dunstan, by Westminster Abbey. When he had removed his cloth cap and entered the palace, he discussed with the Queen the challenge posed to philosophical theology by the loss of so many children's lives in the Aberfan disaster in Wales.

Sometimes when professors have become bishops, there has been a lament that their academic achievement has been exchanged for trivialities. In Ian Ramsey's case in 1966, there was a general feeling among the informed that at the age of fifty-one his main interests were now in pastoral leadership, in administration, and in the application of a Christian philosophy to current problems, rather

[1] See, for example, Ian Ramsey's careful tribute to the working parties on political and moral problems sponsored by the British Council of Churches (*Frontier*, Autumn 1968).

than in systematic metaphysics. And certainly the draft of *Fact, Metaphysics, and God* was to lie untouched in a green cabinet in that yellow study of his in Auckland Castle. But it is clear that Ramsey, whose life had been that of a don, was genuinely alarmed by the job of a diocesan bishop, so much less orderly than running a hospital—particularly when he found that he had to deal with forty letters a day. There is also no doubt that in at least one respect he was sorry to leave Oxford.

He now had a vision that theology could be rejuvenated by dealing with questions such as personal responsibility; crime and punishment; sin, law, and the State; health and healing; education; man's destiny and purpose. He wrote in *Theology* (December 1964): 'It is by wrestling with such problems in a co-operative venture of scholarship with other academic disciplines that theology may find a new prospect and a new relevance.' He was delighted to take part in the 1962 conference sponsored by the Modern Churchmen's Union, resulting in the book *Biology and Personality* (with a 'Personal Retrospect' by Charles Raven, who died in 1964). But he also dreamed of an institute in Oxford to give such discussions a broader and more permanent basis; and he had to leave Oxford for Durham with that part of the vision still unfulfilled.

At the end of *Models and Mystery*, he put his vision into words. 'Here is a view of a university, not as a mere area for power struggles between professional disciplines, still less as a mere setting in which men go about their segregated jobs; here is a university which holds together and harmonises the technical and the humane, the specialization and the broad perspective, the mind which is analytically critical and the person who is broadly sensitive and sympathetic, which holds together understanding and insight, models and mystery.'

He went back to Oxford in 1969, to lead a mission to the university. His talks in the Sheldonian Theatre were above the heads of many of the students and some of the clergy who heard them. Oxford's most popular and effective vicar is said to have emerged muttering, 'isomorphous?' But once again Ian Ramsey's personal qualities shone out, not only in the main meetings, but supremely in the private committee where he was told that he was being too clever and too critical. He took this rebuke so well that some who had been complaining were silenced by the thought that a truly humble man of God was in Oxford.

5

Bishop of Durham

IAN RAMSEY was the ninetieth Bishop of Durham.[1] It was inevitable that he should be compared with the great Victorian scholar-bishops, Lightfoot and Westcott, who had been moved there straight from professorships. But C. J. Stranks, the author of the 1973 history of Durham Cathedral, has observed that the Bishop of Durham most like Ian Ramsey in character was John Cosin (1660-72), who swept through the diocese with a rare determination and energy. Certainly Bishop Ramsey was an activist. It was said of Joseph Butler at Durham (by Horace Walpole) that 'he had been wafted to that see on a cloud of metaphysics and remained absorbed in it', but actually Butler was a practical bishop—and how much more so Ian Ramsey!

The one and a half million people in the diocese in 1966 posed no easy challenge, for Durham Diocese was more conscious of past glories than of present opportunities. Church life reflected a surrounding depression which was largely caused by the contraction of the basic industries of coalmining and shipbuilding. In an article prepared to welcome the 1973 Methodist Conference to Newcastle-upon-Tyne, Ramsey spent most of his time enthusing about the North-East; not for nothing was he President of the Northumbria Tourist Board. But he painted a contemporary picture which most other men would have found gloomy.

Men and women less robust in character, or weaker in personal fibre,

[1] Essays on Bishops Lightfoot, Westcott, and Henson are included in David L. Edwards, *Leaders of the Church of England, 1828-1944* (1971).

or having less inward strength, or a shallower faith, would never have endured. As it is, the struggles of half a century may see for a third generation the dawning of a new day. But even that dawn seems, at the moment, to delay. School-leavers in Sunderland, for example, find it desperately difficult to find jobs; small firms in the dales find it increasingly difficult to pay their way. Some of the lighter industries have catered better for female labour than for men, and so have created more difficulties rather than help solve already existing ones. For while there is nothing exceptional today in both husband and wife working, the North-East miner, for example, finds it demoralising to depend on his wife as wage-earner. Meanwhile, in terms of unemployment, housing, educational, medical and dental services, so deep-seated is its underprivileged character that despite every kind of effort by local and national authorities, there remain huge problems yet to be faced.

The sermon which a new bishop preaches when he has been enthroned in his cathedral is naturally regarded as a declaration of personality, if not of policy. Ian Ramsey's own sermon of this nature, on 15 December 1966, has been recalled by some of the hearers with adjectives such as 'momentous', for it announced the arrival of a man of vision. 'Words, persons, institutions, possess genuine authority as and when they are vehicles of a vision, as and when they disclose that which they are meant to symbolise; and in responding to such an authority as this men find their freedom and life.' His sympathies obviously embraced the young: 'the long hair and the short skirt ... are symbols of protest against what are regarded as the oppressive customs and traditions of an earlier generation'. They also embraced the special problems of the North-East, a long passage of his sermon being an appreciation of recently published *Challenge of the Changing North*, sponsored by the Northern Economic Planning Council. It was a self-disclosure that inaugurated a term of service both Christian and modern. Having been seated in 'the throne which here at Durham, as I am told, is the highest throne in Christendom', the new bishop trusted that 'the authority I exercise will never be incongruous with the Gospel or with conscience or with reason'.

A senior priest who heard that sermon recalls: 'it was evident that we were to have a bishop in new, refreshing, and liberating terms'. And Fred Hurrell, Editor of the *Durham Advertiser*, sums up what Ian Ramsey did. 'He would walk into a social, a meeting, a sports gathering, a tree planting ceremony, so quietly that organizers were often startled to find him there. In talk he never dropped anyone to turn to someone seemingly more important. He just seemed to regard everyone as worth talking to, and everyone took their turn. He soon got on Christian name terms and remembered them marvellously. One thinks of him playing dominoes in a North-West Durham Workmen's Club, dancing with pressmen's wives, being the active president of the League of Friends at Winterton, a large psychiatric hospital. A flame was with us, and light and warmth were there.' Gradually the new bishop—a 'wee' and 'canny' man—was enthroned in the hearts of the reserved and sometimes dour folk of County Durham. Endless stories were told of his concern for individuals and his kindness, but nothing he did made such an impact on the whole diocese as his decision to shake hands at the door with every member of the congregation after almost every service.

On the other hand, as an enthronement sermon Ian Ramsey's had some ominous defects. It was too long. It went into the history of the Bishops of Durham, and of the ceremony of enthronement, in too much detail. Its biblical text (the centurion's saying: 'I also am a man set under authority, having under me soldiers') did not sufficiently unify its contents. Above all, it was too academic. It had no direct message for the discouraged parish priest, or for the layman who had turned up at an ecclesiastical ceremony asking himself how Christianity was relevant to him. As a piece of religious oratory, it was inferior to the sermons collected in, for example, Michael Ramsey's *Durham Essays and Addresses* (1956), notably his enthronement sermon of 1952: 'Members of the Clergy, rejoice that you are privileged to teach his truth, to care for his people, to celebrate the mystery of his body and blood, and to know perhaps his patience and his suffering as you serve him.... Members of the Laity, rejoice that you are privileged to worship.... Rejoice that he asks the whole of your allegiance, that he honours you with the most complete demand upon you.'

Ian Ramsey was conscious of his defects as a preacher. He used to say that it was more difficult to prepare a parochial sermon than a university lecture. He did, however, make great efforts to get his vision across to youngsters being confirmed and to parishioners, and experience improved his performance. His sense of conviction communicated itself, and so did his vision to those with eyes to see.

And at least everyone could see that he had taken trouble. An address when a new incumbent was being instituted into a parish would be crammed with local allusions. These confirmation and institution addresses, which in the mouths of other bishops can become routine, were used by Ian Ramsey to stimulate fresh thought about the meaning of being a Christian, and being a priest, and being the Church. He obviously found something momentous in handing over the Church's heritage and the 'cure' of souls on these occasions. 'For that is what tradition is', he told the clergy assembled in the Convention of York in an address in 1970, '—not the handing down, but the handing over—*traditio*; not the handing down of something which is at all points fixed and final, but the handing over of something which has to show its significance for every day and age.' And what was involved for him in the spoken *traditio* may be seen as the fact that in the last quarter of 1971 he had to prepare 57 original speeches, talks, and sermons excluding confirmation addresses.

But all who had the privilege of discussion with him agreed that he was better out of the pulpit. At his best—and he was frequently at his best—informal discussions including him were memorably illuminating. One priest in a rural part of the diocese writes: 'We all recall the morning in my home when he sat among his clergy answering questions. His brilliance in the intimacy of that small group was complete. But equally I remember his visit to a tiny parish celebrating its centenary. The next day the churchwarden told me there was not a person in that village hall to whom he had not spoken.' On one occasion someone apologized to him for having a bee in his bonnet. 'Oh never mind that,' this extraordinary bishop immediately replied. 'Let the bees buzz—that's how the honey comes.' 'Again and again one would feel exasperated by what Ian said or did, or failed to say or do,' writes a veteran parish priest, 'and then one would be with him, and be fascinated and quite enormously impressed by the goodness of such an astonishing character.'

Fortunately something of the liveliness of his informal utterances is on record in the book *All One Body*, which consisted of reflections on their work by bishops selected from those in London for the Lambeth Conference.[1] The bishops had been interviewed, and their replies recorded. Ian Ramsey's contribution was the longest of the

[1] Ed. Timothy Wilson (1969).

fifty-one. It supplies a more interesting account of his aims than is provided by any of the addresses which he printed in his diocesan magazine, the *Bishoprick*. And it includes a frank statement of his own vocation as he had come to hear it: 'the theologian justifies himself only in terms of the issues and the problems which the world raises.'

He was asked if living in a castle did not make him remote. He replied: 'if one goes to the gate of Auckland Castle where Bishops of Durham have lived for over eight hundred years, one is in the bustle of the market place and very much involved in the world.' But he quickly went on to the vision: 'on one side is park land with a wonderful vision over north Durham ... a view which to me is a perpetual inspiration whether it be early morning or a summer evening.'

This view of Auckland Castle was too romantic to be completely real. As a bishop's home in twentieth-century conditions, the castle is grossly overlarge and highly inconvenient. It is also a monument to feudalism and exploitation, despite the brave talk that it unites the sacred and the secular. When Ramsey went there in 1966, he received advice to move his home to Durham, a dozen miles away. Instead, before his death he had arranged for the diocesan office to move from Durham to Auckland Castle. He over-rode many hesitations because he loved the place, and he was able to do so because his wife devoted herself to running it as an hospitable home without any resident domestic help. She was asked by a visiting electrician if she worked there part time. 'No,' she replied truthfully, 'full time.'

From this combination of the traditional and the contemporary, the vision and the involvement, came in *All One Body* the excited outpouring of a bishop's hopes for State and Church. 'What we want to bring now, not only to society, but even to science, is the idea of each providing opportunities for pioneering ventures. ... The word "static" must have no place at all in our thinking. ... There is much about the present structure of the church which is admirable, but it is a machinery which never seems to work.' *Never?* Bishop Ramsey checked himself: 'with enough determination, one could do a great deal with the present set up.'

What he wanted to do was illustrated from a neighbouring village which was being deserted because of a lack of jobs: Witton Park. 'What is its future? On what grounds do we decide its future?' He did not emphasize the 'we' in that last sentence, but it was breath-taking in comparison with the normal assumption that the Church must remain on the margins of modern society. To Ramsey, the Church 'can be a point around which other disciplines can cluster so as to provide for them a kind of catalyst which might lead to creative decision, or a kind of seeding point around which would crystallise out the solution to a problem'. He gave examples of what could be done by talking about the involvement of many of the clergy in training courses for apprentice miners, and about the newspaper published by the Church to give some cohesion to the new town of Peterlee.

Questioned about church life in *All One Body*, Ramsey said: 'A person is only going to become a priest if he believes that through the Eucharist, and through his part in it, linked as he is with the congregation and representative of the whole Church, there comes a vision of the eternal dimension, the grace and power of God mediated in this way.' The more a priest entered into the concerns of the laity, 'the more his own prayer life would be strengthened. It could not help but be.' Ramsey acknowledged that many forms of worship needed to be updated and he cited with praise the modern prayers of the Frenchman Michael Quoist, made out of 'bank notes and cigarettes and railway tickets and so on'. But he saw 'no blue print'. 'How does one help people with their prayers? Just getting Durham miners to mouth words of prayer is obviously wrong in every way. It seems to me that you won't teach Durham miners (or anyone else) to pray unless you somehow get them first of all to be aware of another dimension to existence. Prayer in the last resort is meditation in the awareness of this extra dimension of God.'

Something of what would be involved in working out a contemporary life was presented in a paper to a conference organized in Durham by the Parish and People Movement.[1] Much of the paper was destructive 'Some Christians have come to realize that well-polished and well-formulated though their theology was, it meant simply nothing, and bore not at all on the world of race-riots, redundancy, over-crowding, juke-boxes, guitars and drugs, motorways, supermarkets...' Much of the paper was critical of those thinkers (he instanced T. R. Miles) who, recognizing the problem, seemed to Ramsey to go too far by abandoning petitionary

[1] Printed in *Spirituality for Today*, ed. Eric James (1968).

prayer to the God who is 'other than myself'. The concluding part
was a plea for silence 'when the activity of God bears on our own'.
'This is the silence to which all theology must point.... To find
such a silence in the Church, in the Cross, in the Bible, in the
Eucharist, is to discover the heart of Christian spirituality.'

A revealing incident occurred when Ramsey was taken off by
Eric James while the conference discussed his lecture in groups.
James expressed admiration and gratitude, but asked what he
would say to Durham miners. Ramsey replied that he would begin
by finding out the man's enthusiasm: it might be for the children,
or for the car. 'Enthusiasm is so often the gateway to adoration!'
The incident was revealing both because Ramsey's answer printed
itself on his companion's memory, and because the question was
necessary. His greatness was that he advocated fresh approaches.
But it was not among his gifts to work out a new way of prayer.

Our Understanding of Prayer was a booklet revised after discussion on the Archbishops' Commission on Christian Doctrine, but
based on one of Ramsey's addresses in the Oxford Mission of 1969.
It provided a richer understanding of the prayer of silence: 'Behold
the handmaid of the Lord!' And of the words of prayer: 'verbal
pathways to a disclosure of God, ... the words should provide us
with reflections appropriate to our being in God's presence, or
describe the circumstances which we offer to God in the hope that
God's saving activity will be disclosed and revealed through them.'
It also tackled the difficult subject of intercessory prayers, 'whose
articulation is for our benefit; they are an offering which brings a
situation before God, hoping his will will match what to us seem
to be the needs'. These are guiding principles which, one would
suppose, are bound to be observed in working out new ways of
prayer, making a time of personal or corporate worship (in
Ramsey's words) 'a point at which our whole life focuses on a
speech-act, a small pattern of words, images, behaviour, and behaviour possibilities, which we hope will be a centre where God
discloses himself and his loving power in Christ'.

What Ramsey advocated in this booklet, he practised in his
diocese. His senior clergy would say to each other that meetings
were made worthwhile by the bishop's introductory prayers, which
were never an arid formula. 'With him', writes one, 'there was the
quiet concentration; the sense of genuine, unhurried attention.
One felt that here was a man who in simplicity of heart, yet with

the entire integration of his whole mature personality, communed with God on the basis of humble trust and complete dedication.' Nor was this ability to communicate a religious disclosure confined to formal worship. Bishop Kenneth Skelton recalled after his death: 'When I visited him in hospital he was lying in a little ward with virtually no outlook. But he told me of his joy at being able to watch the light from the street lamp shining on the wet twigs of a tree just outside his window. Light—and growth—and a pattern: there to the eye of faith were a glimpse of God.'

Our Understanding of Prayer was, however, not really intended for those who never prayed—or for those who would be baffled by Ramsey's acceptance of the miracle of turning water into wine. Inevitably, he had most to say to the clergy who shared his own acceptance of the Church, the Cross, the Bible, the Eucharist, and a devout silence.

On several occasions he delivered a lecture on 'The Theology of Priesthood' which has, however, not yet been printed. It was full of biblical references and theological learning, but its themes were clear.

The priest is one who is a representative person, holy, specially related to God in particular by actively offering certain things—sacrifices—to God in order to create wholeness, roundness, to point men to perfection and to help them to attain it.... In Christ on the Cross all the ingredients of priestly activity were together and united—the priest, the victim, humanity, and God himself. In this way the old priestly dispensation was rounded off.... But how would the new priest then be introduced? ... In so far as the Eucharist, the Lord's Supper, proclaims and makes clear the Lord's death—discloses through bread broken and wine poured the love and power of God in Christ—here is something which can disclose the eternal sacrifice.... When we say that a priest shares in the priesthood of Christ that is a compact way of saying that by being linked with the bread and wine of the sacrament, he models and points to that activity of God in Christ.... What do we make of the priesthood of all believers? ... As Christ offered himself and gave his life a ransom for many, as a shepherd cared for the sheep, interceded with the Father, so also those who are members of Christ's Body.

Such teaching did much to reassure those who thought that Ramsey was too prone to overpraise the efficiency of the secular world (at the expense of what he would tactlessly call the ecclesiastical 'machine'). Yet it was probably too abstract to be completely helpful to most priests—and some 380 clergy in Durham Diocese looked on Bishop Ramsey as their Father-in-God.

It was not that he lacked sympathy with a parish priest's difficulties. While an Oxford professor, he made time to attend the meetings in Westminster of the Board of the Clergy Friendly Society, which exists to help with financial problems. When Pamela Hansford Johnson (Lady Snow) wanted to write a novel about the loneliness and distress of a parson, she turned to Ian Ramsey as the clergyman who had officiated at her wedding, and she did not turn in vain; in ninety minutes or so, Ramsey poured out advice which did much to inform *The Humbler Creation* (1959). When as Bishop of Durham he became responsible pastorally for some priests who got into deep waters of debt or mental distress, he treated them with endless compassion. One—a former curate, then in a psychiatric hospital—recalls a letter of encouragement written from a station waiting-room in Canada. When a clergyman seemed to a diocesan committee unduly awkward, Ramsey tended to classify him as the underdog and to protect him. Other clergy remember the trouble taken by their bishop to share their normal happiness and sorrows.

But he never completely overcame the suspicions which many of the clergy have towards academics. Owing to a lack of experience in charge of a parish, he left the impression that he could not see just how humble and testing, but rewarding, a part of the creation a parish can be. Owing to his many preoccupations, he often had to ask clergy to wait days or even weeks for appointments. If the matter was urgent, a parish priest would be fitted in between engagements or would be visited late in the evening. And because of his deep-rooted conviction that adults should make up their own minds, he would not dispense practical tips about how to run a parish. Instead he would discuss the principles involved. Just as philosophers had complained that he was a priest, so now priests complained that he was a philosopher.

On the other hand, the fact that Ramsey had a vision wider than the conventional parish could have a bracing effect. He taught that priests had something to learn as well as something to teach in dialogue with those who practised the skills of medicine or the social services. He was chairman of both the groups, one convened by the British Council of Churches and the other by the Institute of Religion and Medicine, which published their discussions and recommendations in the report *Pastoral Care and the Training of*

Ministers (1968)—a report annotated in draft so extensively in Ramsey's writing that the secretary (G. C. Harding) had to buy a magnifying glass. He lectured 'On Not Being Judgemental' to the Scottish Pastoral Association in 1969, and reprinted the lecture for his own clergy in the *Bishoprick* (August 1970). He praised the 'acceptance' practised by social workers 'when we realize that the image of the Church is often judgemental in the bad sense, we also realise what an appallingly difficult task lies ahead of us'. But in a careful criticism of Jean Heywood's book on *Casework and Pastoral Care*, he was equally insistent that the Church must preserve the categories of right and wrong. 'In judging an action wrong or a situation evil, we do not necessarily blame anyone.'

Bernard Sharp, who went to Africa after a curacy in the diocese of Durham, has summed up the influence on the responsive clergy. 'He was to me a dearly loved father, caring deeply for the whole man, personally concerned about one's ideas, feelings, and problems. From him I learned to accept difficulties squarely, and to value both study and personal contact with all sorts of people. I also learned to see the work of God around us in the world today.'

On the whole, he was a layman's bishop. The kind of activity he most enjoyed was a regular discussion with police officers about their problems. As he observed in *Only One Body*, 'most of my life has been spent in the company of laymen—admittedly in the rather specialist communities of universities and schools and teaching generally. One does know ... that clergy look at things very differently from their lay counterparts.... What I am saying is that besides involvement in personal crises like birth, marriage and death, the clergyman has to be involved as far as he can be in other social areas.' So he often spoke to the clergy about 'outreach'—a favourite word which often irritated priests who felt they had been reaching out all their lives. He also believed strongly that the laity should answer the clergy back. When in the service instituting a new incumbent in a parish the congregation was told, 'it is the duty of the people to learn the Christian faith by reading and meditation', he always added, with emphasis: 'and by argument and discussion'.

Articles or addresses printed in the *Bishoprick* record parts of the vision which he held up before the layman out of church. In May 1968 lengthy reflections on an urban, technological society were sparked off by Harvey Cox's book, *The Secular City*. Although 'we can be appalled by what is the narrowness, the blindness of so much of our thinking and planning today', and although 'it is very easy indeed to dismiss the whole of religion and theology as a sham, the Church as a community of the immature', these reflections were full of faith. 'The industrial life and social patterns which in themselves foster anonymity can, if properly used, afford precisely the background of varied possibilities and the conditions for dynamic economic growth within which a person can find freedom and fullness of life. It is only when we have learned to tie a white bow-tie "mechanically", anonymously, that we have extra time in which to discover more dynamic and exciting pursuits for the evening's entertainment.'

In August 1971 he was still optimistic when he printed the address he had just given to the Durham Miners' Gala. He praised the history of the miners' struggle, and the strength of their present-day characters and skills. He praised consultation and negotiation as the 'civilized way' of the mining industry (this was in the year before the national miners' strike). He urged: 'What we need to do is to transform this industrial region by all the developments and resources which modern technology can afford us.' He pleaded for partnership between workers and management as 'something that in the future can win men's loyalty and dedication, as did the battle against injustice and victimisation in the past'.

The fullest statement he ever made to laymen of his vision of a new culture—'scientific, moral, religious, and technological at the same time'—came in a lecture to the Royal Society for the Encouragement of Arts, Manufacturers, and Commerce in 1971. It was the lay equivalent of his eighty-minute address on the 'Crisis of Faith' which both stunned and stimulated the Church Leaders' Conference at Birmingham in 1972, five weeks before his death.[1]

The Royal Society which Ramsey addressed has—or so he claimed—'always stood for science being used for the benefit of society by being wedded with moral insights and made part of a religious quest'. He recalled some of the founders in 1752: Hogarth, John Howard, Chippendale, Robert Adam. He extolled this high noon of the eighteenth century at some length (and with some extravagance), and mentioned the thing which had perhaps first awakened his enthusiasm for it: Roubiliac's statue of Newton in

[1] See David L. Edwards, *The British Churches Turn to the Future* (1973), pp. 32-8.

Trinity College Chapel in Cambridge. He told the sad story of the
break-up of this unity. 'It was philosophers like Descartes, Hume,
and Kant whose ideas encouraged men ... to break into a thousand
pieces that harmony between science and religion which Newton's
statue expressed.... Theology was content to be, and even desired
to be, a subject apart.... It was all too easy for science to become
pure science and for industry and technology to develop independently—the only aim being the greatest possible financial profit.'
And he emphasized how the universities had stood aloof, citing
Newman's conviction that it was the business of a university not to
teach 'some temporal calling, or some mechanical art, or some
physical secret' but to train gentlemen.

Yet this lecture voiced all Ramsey's optimism. The points, now
familiar to his admirers but not to the businessmen who heard
him that evening in London, were all made. 'The influence of technology on society proved irresistibly powerful'—but so, too, did the
conscience of mankind, appalled by dangers of a technology un-
directed by humane and social considerations. Ramsey recalled how
a Rector of Jarrow had begged Sir Humphrey Davey to invent a
lamp that miners could use with safety; and how in the contemporary world it was becoming more and more outrageous that the
Russian engineer in charge of the building of the Aswan Dam, when
asked about the consequences for the environment, had replied:
'My job is just to build the dam.' And once again Ramsey said:
'the time is ripe for inter-professional, inter-disciplinary study' to
produce 'balanced decisions and a technology of fulfilment and
release'.

He saw clearly that the Christian approach to social problems and
opportunities of this magnitude must be more than denominational.
In 1970 he gathered, and at first presided over, the North-East
Ecumenical Group, a bi-monthly gathering of bishops (both
Anglican and Roman Catholic) with leaders of the Free Churches
from the Tweed to the Tees. This not only led to unprecedented
personal contacts but also tackled many problems of co-operation,
including 'Action North-East', a distinctive share in the 'Call to the
North' evangelistic campaign initiated by the Archbishop of York
in 1972-3. The NEEG gave birth in its turn to a group on social
responsibility. Further projects seemed on the eve of commissioning
on an ecumenical basis when Ramsey died. One was a Pastoral

Institute for both clergy and laity under the auspices of Durham University. Another was a training course in pastoral counselling to meet more practical needs. A vital reason for these developments has been put succinctly by the Methodist leader, Kenneth Waights: 'Ian Ramsey had the rare quality of being a man greater than his office.'

But was his strategy greater than his office work? Did he have a strong policy for his diocese? In his first Presidential Address to the Diocesan Conference, on a warm, sunny afternoon in June 1967, it certainly sounded as if he had.

He spoke of the need of a 'broad pattern' in deploying the clergy whether in parochial or specialist work—and of an 'overall policy' about stipends. 'I am hoping very soon to announce a plan which will take care of the recruitment and training of clergy for the diocese, as well as make provisions for their first and subsequent appointments in the early years of their ministry.... The need is there for some kind of group, for the moment informal and experimental, with whom I can consult, and with whose help I can formulate broad issues of policy.... On Tuesday and Wednesday of this week I visited some twenty-four areas containing new estates and new towns, and I am hoping ... to be able to formulate some policy in relation to staffing, churches, halls, and other amenities, possible patterns of ministry, co-operation with other churches, and similar issues.' He even spoke of the need of a 'great amount of delegation' in order that his correspondence might be dealt with more efficiently.

In the event, Ramsey was criticized both for being obstinate and even autocratic in pressing ideas which seemed revolutionary and for failing to push necessary reforms through. It is the custom in the Church of England to shoot from both these directions at bishops, who are consecrated to be sacrificial victims. But special factors were at work in Ian Ramsey's case.

Specially when so tired towards the end of his life, he talked too much at meetings. He would answer from the chair almost every point made in discussion. He would also fuss over details—the ordering of a service or the building of a house: the service must be perfect, to the glory of God, and likewise the new Vicarage. He did delegate some matters, but not enough. On the other hand, he was in some ways thought to be too democratic. Committees were convened to debate questions which probably one man ought to have decided, perhaps by tossing a coin. The minutes of these meetings received the personal attention which, it may be, ought to have been given to the completion of *Fact, Metaphysics, and God.* And enthusiasts were told that a diocese could have no policy; that a bishop must simply do the next thing that came along. What was certainly true was that this bishop had too many things to do. In the circumstances, the administration could not be ideal. Weeks would pass without letters being answered. Major experiments might be inaugurated by trusting someone to draw up his (or her) own job-description and get on with it. Appointments could be offered after surprisingly few soundings—although, it is said, some of the most risky were turned down by the men first invited, since not everyone shared Ramsey's own appetite for improbable adventures. And his failure to probe deeply into the problems involved meant that some of his ideas never got off the ground. There was talk about bringing the Divinity Faculty at Durham more firmly into the workaday life of the North-East. There was talk about co-ordinating the chaplaincy work among the students. There was talk about rearranging the boundaries with the dioceses of Newcastle and York, and perhaps creating a new diocese or two.

It is right to record these criticisms as showing the kind of problems, in himself or others, out of which Ramsey's achievement as a diocesan bishop began to emerge. But it would be ridiculous to imply that criticism prevailed over the general conviction that a lovable saint was among them; or that everything depended on the bishop's own strengths and weaknesses. Inevitably the life of a diocese depends in large measure on the people around the bishop— a group which often he has inherited. In Durham's case there was Alec Hamilton, the Suffragan Bishop of Jarrow, who had spent his life as a parish priest. There was Cecil Ferens, legal secretary to the Bishops of Durham since 1929. There was Phyllis Carter, who ran the diocesan office as her father had done before her. And there were two friends brought into the diocese as aides: Michael Perry, the exceptionally able and young Archdeacon of Durham, and Harry McClatchey, who had been in personnel management before a late ordination, and who now combined a parish with the duties of Bishop's Chaplain.

Given more time, Ramsey could have used his energy and prestige to follow up systematically many reforms which he intro-

duced. One example of his forward-looking drive was his encouragement of various 'group' (or even more closely knit 'team')
ministries, drawing the parish clergy out of isolation. Another was
the regular council where the unbeneficed clergy let off steam in
unprecedented freedom.

Another was his emphasis that every clergyman, not only those
recently ordained, needed further training. Again breaking with all
precedent, he appointed Miss Mollie Batten, Dame Enid Russell-
Smith, and a London psychiatrist, Dr. R. F. Hobson, together with
the usual dons as his 'examining' chaplains. Once a year they met
in Auckland Castle for a free debate in which curates or rural
deans might find themselves involved. In addition he appointed
a Ministry Committee to meet regularly under the Bishop of Jarrow,
and to be served by a Director of Further Training and a Recruitment Officer together with two assistants and a Finance Officer. At
the time, no other diocese in England was making such great efforts
to secure future parsons and to develop their potentialities once
ordained.

He took an early stand on the importance of specialist ministries
such as the Tees-side Industrial Mission (formally constituted under
an agreement signed by him with the Archbishop of York and the
Methodist Chairman in 1967). Bill Wright, the leader of this work,
writes:

At first Ian Ramsey didn't know much about industry—but he picked
it up! Within a couple of years he was chairing a half-day consultation
of ninety representatives of organizations interested in public participation in planning, meeting the key speakers over lunch, ranging round
a dozen work-groups picking up their ideas, conflating all this material,
and then pushing the meeting miles ahead of its own assumed ability.
Whatever the issue, he was able to repeat this kind of performance.
When he died there were seven clergy in the Durham diocese in full-time
mission in industry, and we were working towards a new style of lay
education (Christian Urban Exploration). Ian gave his wholehearted
support. And whenever I impatiently wanted him to crowd more
support for our experiments into his programme, he was thoroughly
open and made it impossible for me not to be straight with him.

In 1969 he appointed Miss Margaret Kane, who had been working
in Hong Kong, as his 'theological consultant' on industrial and
social affairs, and he backed up her work all over the North-East,
stimulating discussions. However, he did not escape private criti-

cism from some in industrial management who felt that he had
identified himself too readily with the workers, and had not paid
enough attention to the problems of management. Nor did it go
unremarked that some of the discussions sponsored by the industrial mission seemed to be based on the day's newspaper rather than
on the New Testament.

The parochial clergy naturally tended to be suspicious of the
'sector ministries' which developed in the diocese—of, for example,
the able and attractive priest who was freed to do pastoral work
in the clubs and Bingo halls of Tees-side and (perhaps worse still)
to encourage local young people to be artists. Much of the income of
the clergy comes nowadays through block grants to each diocese
from the Church Commissioners, who control almost all the inherited endowments, and Ramsey persuaded Durham Diocese to
pay a substantial part of this money to the specialist or sector clergy.
He was attracted by the argument that this reflected the original
intention of the Church of England's benefactors for the religious
and general welfare of the people of England. Many of the parish
clergy felt the routine of worship, clubs, and visiting to be vastly
more important and more worth financing than what seemed the
bishop's pet schemes. Ramsey spent too little time in taking such
feelings seriously. But he saw no necessary conflict between the
parishes and the sectors. Indeed, he loved to devise schemes to use
part of the time (and income) of the incumbent of a small parish
in work for the diocese as a whole.

What sometimes seemed in County Durham to be Ian Ramsey's
own radical notions were in those years being put into practice in
many parts of the Church of England. When an independent commission appointed by Ramsey made a study of church life in Sunderland—a detailed study which took two years—it recommended
in its elaborate report (*The Church in Sunderland*, 1971) that an
industrial mission should be created and that at least part of the
time of several parish priests should be given to specialist activities
covering the whole town, as Social Responsibility Officer, Public
Relations Officer, and Chaplain for the Arts and Recreation (and
also as Religious Education specialist and Community Development
Officer, if the local authority did not make these two appointments
itself). The remaining full-time parish priests should be reorganized
with these specialists, to form a single team under a local bishop's
leadership; the parishes should no longer be independent. Ramsey's

preface to this report greeted it as 'thorough, well-informed, practical, and realistic'. It could be suggested that the bishop had put
on the commission only people likely to agree with his radical
approach; on the other hand, the group included a local industrial-
ist and a trade unionist, with the Archdeacon of Northumberland
from the next diocese, and was chaired by Dame Enid Russel-
Smith.

Before becoming Principal of St. Aidan's College, Durham,
Dame Enid had been a senior civil servant. She writes:

I first really met Ian Ramsey in the spring of 1969 when he was setting
up his commission on the Church in Sunderland. The characteristic
which impressed me most was his confidence. The questions the commission would have to consider were difficult and the inquiry itself
might be resented in Sunderland but having chosen the members with
great care—and people with national reputations were ready to travel
long distances to work for him—he was happy to leave us to get on with
the job. It never seemed to enter his head that we might make a mess
of it. This kind of confidence begets confidence in those who are the
subject of it, and was perhaps the main reason why the commission's
courage remained so high and individual members were willing to take
on some very onerous tasks.

Dr. Ramsey showed at this time another quality which I did not
fully recognize until much later: an insight into the way people's minds
work, which was, I suppose, wisdom. When I found that he was going
to surround the commission with a galaxy of no less than six local
committees which were all to complete inquiries into various aspects of
life in Sunderland before the commission could report, I thought we were
faced with an unmanageable administrative nightmare. But by the end
of the inquiry, when cross-fertilization had taken place in both directions, the local committee members were enthusiastic missionaries for
many of the most radical of the commission's recommendations which
were themselves often based on the committees' own suggestions. Dr.
Ramsey must, I think, have seen from the start that this would take
place, while I was short-sightedly preoccupied with the risk of unbridgeable divisions of opinion.

These two qualities of confidence to act and wise far-sightedness are
perhaps the essence of leadership, and leadership he certainly had. Every
time I met him I was surprised to see how small he was. As with other
truly 'big' men, it is difficult to say what made up this quality. It lay
more in what he was than in what he said. When talking to him, I used
to feel that there was often no need to tell him much, for he knew it all
already. He had the gift, sometimes seen in politicians, of deducing

implications from the mere mention of a first principle. This made it so easy to explain anything to him, and his quickness to grasp an idea was remarkable.

It was cruelly ironic that, understanding so easily points of administration and organization when presented to him for instance in connection with the Sunderland Commission, he should have found it so difficult to organize his own work on lines which did not impose on him an intolerable personal load. He was perhaps too lacking in the instinct for self-preservation, too self-sacrificing to refuse commitments, and he never seems to have learned to delegate. The art of delegation involves an attitude of mind which an academic career may do little to develop in a young man, and it is very difficult to acquire suddenly in middle age. He was also perhaps too impatient to get on with the work to give enough time to the lengthy business of letting people know what is happening and to preliminary consultations, which can save a lot of time and trouble in later stages. The tragedy is that these relatively minor limitations must have contributed to the situation which killed him.

So this episcopate was cut short before it could come to full fruition. But we may conclude with some words written to the Duchess of Somerset by Bishop Joseph Butler when that philosopher had busied himself with improvements to Auckland Castle and had felt 'the burlesque of being employed in this manner at my time of life'. Butler wrote: 'But in another view, and taking in all circumstances, these things, trifling as they may appear, no less than things of greater importance, seem to be put upon me to do, or at least to begin; whether I am to live to complete any or all of them, is not my concern.'

6

To the Limits

In the Middle Ages the Bishop of Durham guarded England against the Scots. But while at Durham, Ian Ramsey had his eyes on the frontier between the Church and the world.

He was fascinated by the secular world, as some of his clergy complained; rather, he felt compelled to relate the Christian Gospel to every area of secular life which he could reach. Not for nothing had his philosophical writings more than once contrasted the routine behaviour of the priest and Levite with the genuinely personal response of the Samaritan to a fellow-man's need. The physical efforts involved in so many journeys and meetings cost him more than oil, wine, and two *denarii*. But we should not forget that intellectual efforts were also needed, for Ian Ramsey was not one who thought that all the solutions to the many problems involved were already printed in the Bible or in some other textbook. He already knew the Christian perspective on life as a whole, and he got to know many of the detailed problems; but his heart and mind, like his body, had to be stretched to the limits to bring the perspective and the problems together. He wrote at the end of *Christian Ethics and Contemporary Philosophy*: 'What the Christian must do in order to work out a Christian morality in some problematic situation is to set various possible behaviour patterns alongside the Christian perspective ... and see which is the best fit.'

One of the places where he tried to see this was the House of Lords. The Bishop of Durham—together with the Archbishops of Canterbury and York, the Bishops of London and Winchester,

and about half the Church of England's other diocesan bishops in
order of their consecration—is a member of the Upper House.
Historically the reason is that bishops used to be feudal magnates.
Later on the bishops' votes were valued and expected by the political
parties which had appointed them. In modern times the tradition
is questioned, both by those who dislike seeing so many clergymen
of one denomination with a potential influence as members of
Parliament, and by those who are doubtful about the importance
of the Lords and who dislike such distractions from diocesan duties,
even though most of the bishops who are members do a week of
duty reading the prayers which begin the Lords' daily proceedings.

Hensley Henson, in his retrospect of his episcopate between the
world wars, wrote: 'The Bishop of Durham ... is exempt from the
obligation of reading prayers. This I regretted because it deprived
me of a respectable excuse for absenteeism from my diocese.... It
had been my intention and desire to attend the debates with some
regularity. I had not realised ... the practical impossibility of
combining a faithful fulfilment of episcopal duty in Durham with
any regular parliamentary activity in Westminster.... In effect,
I had to choose between Durham and London, and I chose the
course which, from a merely selfish point of view, was least attractive.' But Ramsey refused to acknowledge that any choice was
necessary. Indeed, when in 1966 friends asked him why he was
leaving academic life the first thing he tended to say was that it
had been put to him that the Church of England needed a fresh
spokesman on moral issues in the Lords. He tried to be in the House
every Wednesday, when the debates on general motions were
normally held.

He was introduced into the House on 6 December 1966, but did
not speak in a debate until seven months later. This maiden speech
showed his strength and weakness. His strength lay in the honesty
and ability with which he related Christian ethics to the moral problems of the day—in this first case, abortion. His weakness was that
he was not a professional Parliamentarian, giving and taking knocks
in detailed discussions over the years and slowly acquiring an
instinct for what was, or was not, effective debating and practical
politics. Ironically (because the preparation and travel involved
took so much out of his life), he spoke too often and too long by
the Lords' standards. He did not escape the accusations which peers
tend to mutter against the bishops in their House: that they either

lecture or preach. Although the trade unionists were delighted that a bishop could talk so much sense, the stuffier Tories were dismayed that one could be so controversial—and at such length. A Liberal, Lord Beaumont of Whitley contributes this deliberately unsentimental assessment:

That almost funny little figure on the bishops' bench definitely impressed the House. Reading through his speeches after his death, it is sometimes difficult to see why. Some of his major speeches were very much 'on the one hand ... on the other hand' and came to little constructive conclusion. He was inclined to intervene in debates when he found himself in the House without adequate preparation and almost always made a bad speech when he did. But even when he was not at his best, he came over as a person speaking with authority. He certainly earned the respect and affection of the whole House.

The debate in July 1967 was about an Abortion Bill which was largely but not completely in accordance with the recommendations of the Church of England group which Ramsey had chaired. He therefore welcomed the intention to legalize more abortions while granting the rights of doctors and nurses not to take part in operations against their consciences. 'The only reliable way to combine sensitivity and compassion with a due reasonableness and a wide ranging concern is sure to provide for these sad cases in the context of the mother, so that we ask: is it the best of all possibilities or not that this mother in these circumstances should risk this birth? Can the mother in these circumstances have the customary duty of bringing the child to birth?' But he abstained from voting, and both in the debate and at the later committee stage he tried to amend the Bill so as to provide for more genuine consultation in cases where decisions were difficult. He urged that the family doctor, a psychiatrist, or a medical or psychiatric social worker should be brought into the decision alongside the gynaecologist. And here he failed, partly because his amendment and his manner of presenting it were not fully expert.

Lord Longford, a Roman Catholic, paid tribute to 'the profoundly constructive speech from a great theologian'. And it was more than the conventional encouragement to a maiden speaker when Longford went on to say: 'I hope we shall hear from him very often, because this is possibly the only legislative chamber in the world where theology is positively fashionable.'

Even those in his diocese who resented their bishop's too frequent visits to Westminster were proud that in him the North-East had a champion. A considerable number of Ramsey's interventions in the Lords defended the interests of workers for whom he was pastorally responsible. He urged that more government efforts should be made to open factories in the North-East; and, in the interests of the miners, attacked the incoherence of the nation's fuel policy in February 1968. He even asked a parliamentary question about the Durham police's radio system, which interfered with the reception of B.B.C. programmes. His last speech in the Lords drew attention to the need to subsidize the arts in the regions. He then recalled 'cultural traditions which in a past age represented the total response of man to his environment: linking work, home, recreation, the cobblestones, the whippets, the rivers and the slag heaps and the moorlands'. More vaguely, he wanted new 'art forms' to be developed around the new chemical industries, or around the new technology in the manufacture of steel, as the nation, and particularly the North, worked 'towards the new culture of which so many of our struggles today are but the birth pangs'.

Such enthusiasm from a Bishop of Durham did much to answer the problem implied in a memory which he included in this speech on 22 March 1972. 'I recall seeing Durham Cathedral some forty years ago, for the first time, from a train, as do so many, and wondering what it stood for to the people around it. There, with its castle on the rock, was it integrated with what were then the smoking chimneys of the houses below?'

But Ramsey also defended the rights of all workers to larger shares in the shaping of their working and living conditions; and the rights of young people to protest against what they thought wrong in society. In two speeches in 1969 he pleaded for 'the local initiative which must be at the heart of all democracy' and complained that 'we have done little, very little indeed, to ensure that policies and decisions make evident their moral basis'. He alleged that 'many rejections of appeals connected with planning give the impression of nothing better than stereotyped, routine, ready-made rejections that have made no serious attempt to grapple with particular difficulties'. 'I believe', he said, 'that demonstrations at their best witness to the ever-restless spirit of man.' In the previous year he had defended some of the motives, although not the actions, of young drug-takers, who 'often do this as a means of self-discovery in a world where contemplation and privacy are all at a discount; or it is done as a search for identity in a world of stereotypes ... in a world of shibboleths'. Positively, he suggested that each region should have its own *ombudsman* (investigator of complaints) 're-sponsible only to the Crown'.

Some of Ramsey's contributions to debates sought to arouse more informed sympathy for people glamourized less often than demon-strators and drug-takers. Perhaps the most moving speech he made in the Lords was on 28 January 1970, and concerned the problems of the retired. He quoted from a recent book on the *Psychology of Human Ageing*, but clearly his own concern had been aroused by 'the picture of the man who suddenly discovers overnight that his skill, his energy, his capacity to make rapid decisions, are no longer needed by anybody: he is retired and virtually dead'. He urged that psychologists should give much more attention to the problems of growing old, and that many more efforts should be made to prepare managers and workers for retirement, suggesting that it would be more sensible for people to retire at an age when they were still physically and mentally able to pick up new interests.

Another powerful speech initiated a debate on 17 February 1971 on the problems of long-term prisoners. He saw this concern as a duty which resulted in part from his ardent support of the abolition of hanging, and in part from the fact that Durham Prison had a specially well-known top security wing. He had visited Durham Prison; 'from what I can judge there is little that is satisfying about mailbag work'. And he had studied other evidence. He did not hesitate to repeat to their Lordships from the *TV Times* the case of a prisoner, guilty of a sexual offence against a child, who would find salt or someone's spittle in his cocoa—and would feel that this would go on for unending years. 'What we do in our prisons', he now affirmed, 'must reflect both our opposition to crime on the one hand and our moral evaluation of personality on the other.' (In the 1969 debate on the death penalty, he had said: 'I would remind your Lordships that the only deterrent which in the long run brings any success at all is the power—may I say the inspiration?—of a moral ideal; and it must be a punishment which at the same time makes rehabilitation possible.') To this end, he once again urged the value of an inter-disciplinary group, this time composed of judges, magistrates, lawyers, police, and social workers with probation, medical, and prison officers, to study jointly the problems of long-term prisoners.

He felt intensely for those who were imprisoned in injustice by the colour of their skins. He attacked *apartheid* and expressed sympathy with African liberation movements (although 'for myself I should prefer to be killed rather than to kill'). His description of South Africa House in Trafalgar Square remained in the memories of his hearers. 'Seen in the warm, orange light of the evening it can speak, at first sight attractively, of beauty and order and prosperity. But look at it in the cold, hard light of a winter's day and it is indeed a whited sepulchre, built over a grave containing the bones and aspirations of countless Africans.' He denounced the 1971 proposals for the future of Rhodesia. 'I honestly look in vain for concrete evidence of a radical change of heart on the part of the Rhodesian Government. Yet in my opinion, without that change of heart the proposals before us are bound to be stultified.' He also initiated a debate about the opportunities for multi-racial education, with special reference to the teaching of religion in British schools. 'Our problem is to reconcile deep localised attachments with wider loyalties', but he claimed that 'the Ukrainians in Yorkshire or the Arabs in South Shields' showed what could be done, and he also told their Lordships about a girl he had seen in Chicago one St. Patrick's Day. She was a black girl dressed in green and orange, and she bore a huge label: 'Kiss me, I'm Irish'.

Some of the problems before the Lords were of the kind where a bishop was expected to speak. Thus Ramsey criticized an abortive Bill to legalize euthanasia (although saying that 'if there is any doubt whatever about the legality of withdrawing artificial means of survival when a considered medical-moral decision judges it to be right ... no doubt this is something which needs seriously following up'). He spoke in favour of the 1969 Divorce Reform Bill, while pleading that the state should give more help to poor divorced people.

But other problems which Ramsey saw as equally moral were issues where many urged caution on bishops. He attacked the Conservative policy about incomes and prices (which was changed after his death). 'The public will surely never support, on the one hand, an incomes policy that bites and, on the other hand, a prices policy which has virtually no teeth at all, even artificial teeth.' And on 6 April 1971 he delivered the bravest speech of his career, attacking the Conservatives' Industrial Relations Bill, which he said ought to have been called an 'Industrial Disputes (Regulation of Practices) Bill'. He spoke eloquently of the need to work out human relations in a creative partnership, instead of legislating in 'a desperate hurry after 150 years'. He wanted a much fuller 'code of practice' in industry than anything the Government had in mind. It should include training in industrial relations by day release for shop stewards and by joint management-union schemes. It should provide for access by every worker to joint consultative machinery and to intelligible accounts showing his company's financial status. And the worker should hear all this 'directly from his manager and in his natural work group, with opportunities for discussion'.

Such interventions in economic debates were, in Ramsey's view, necessary parts of moral leadership. 'What we have, if I may speak from the touchline, is a competition and a race where the last thing the contestants know is where they are going and what they are running for, except that each wants to be ahead of the others.... We are nearing bankruptcy in the ideas and moral ideals which stir men's deepest loyalties and which in the last resort, alone will give cohesion to society.... This is no fanciful and impractical idealism of a right reverend prelate; it is the implicit conviction of the ordinary man or woman, up there in County Durham or elsewhere, who wonders where it is all going to end.'

Those contributions to the work of the Lords fulfilled and exceeded the hopes surrounding Ramsey's elevation to the bishops' bench. When he was made Bishop of Durham, it was also expected that he would give theological leadership from a bench which was admitted to lack intellectual distinction. Thus he played a prominent (although not over-prominent) role in the Lambeth Conference of 1968. He was Vice-Chairman of Section 1, on 'The Renewal of the Church in Faith', and drafted much of that part of the Lambeth Report. He also edited the popular summary of Lambeth 1968, *Faith Alert*. Brother-bishops observed that when calling upon the new Bishop of Durham to speak, Archbishop Michael Ramsey's face would betray eagerness instead of the emotions normally apparent. But while Michael Ramsey had been Bishop of Durham,[1] he had secured many hours by himself in his study with his books. Ian Ramsey's episcopal work as a teacher of

[1] 1952-6. He had been succeeded by Maurice Harland, 1956-66.

theology fell into a very different pattern—and not only because he accepted invitations to lecture in most parts of England, in Canada, and in the U.S.A.

The Archbishops of Canterbury and York announced on 22 March 1967 the appointment of a commission 'to consider and advise upon doctrinal questions submitted to it from time to time by the Archbishops and to plan, when desirable, the investigation of questions by other groups'. The plan had grown from a letter sent to a number of theologians by the Archbishop of Canterbury three months previously, recalling the Doctrinal Commission which had last met in 1937. Archbishop Ramsey had made clear in this letter the priorities in mind for any new commission. He had written:

It is evident that the theological tasks of today are very different from those of the period between the wars; for instance a commission appointed today would not be able to start with a similar body of philosophical assumptions and it would find itself concerned not only with the content of what is believed but also with the nature of belief and the character of religious statements. Yet I find a good many people who share my own concern about two needs of the Church of England. One need is that the apparent lack of theological coherence in our Church should be studied with a view to discovering what degree of coherence really does exist and giving expression to it. Another need is that difficulties felt about subscription to formularies should be examined, together with the place and authority of the Thirty-nine Articles.

Disagreement was built into the structure of this commission. Of eighteen members, two (A. M. Allchin and C. P. M. Jones) could be guaranteed to speak for a Catholic view, and two (Michael Green and J. I. Packer) for an Evangelical one. There were, however, also two regarded as radically modern (David Jenkins and Hugh Montefiore), and two laymen who were professional philosophers (John Lucas and Ninian Smart). There were three who were, or became, chiefly known for their attempts to construct a fairly non-controversial restatement of Christianity (J. A. Baker, Howard Root, E. J. Tinsley), and five professors bound to insist on the most rigorous standards (Henry Chadwick, C. F. Evans, D. E. Nineham, H. E. W. Turner, Maurice Wiles). And even these rough classifications give little idea of the diversity of the group (further diversified as membership changed slightly over the years). To some, the salvation of theology seemed to lie in a humbler apprehension of a great tradition going back to the Bible; to others, in a humbler encounter with contemporary knowledge and experience; to more, in both directions. In several ways the group was untypical of the Church of England as a whole. It contained no one who despised theology, no one wedded to the conventional, and no one unwilling to listen and learn. More lamentably, the only parish priest was the vicar of the university church at Cambridge. But a check on its proceedings was provided by the need to submit any of its recommendations which involved changes in the practice of the Church to the Church Assembly (after 1970 to the General Synod). In that legislative body, both conservativism and ignorance were represented.

It was generally agreed six years later that a diocesan bishop had been needed as first chairman; and that since the Archbishop of Canterbury could scarcely have led a body reporting to himself, no one except Ian Ramsey could have achieved the results which had come. As Professor Turner writes: 'He had the striking gift of being able to distil in a sentence or two the real point of a long, somewhat heated, and sometimes rather muddled contribution. He was always scrupulously fair even to minority points of view. He had the gift of respecting the integrity of other people as he valued his own. Perhaps his main weakness was to present disagreements as differences about terms rather than about things. But at all times positive and usually illuminating and clarifying, his aim was to reconcile and to integrate.'

Professor Wiles confirms this verdict:

I don't think he had to force himself to be fair to the ultra conservatives. Surprisingly he seemed to find it a little harder to bear with the ultra radicals—I think because they were inclined to say that some of the issues were unimportant and could be by-passed, or that on some issues attitudes were so incompatible they could not be properly bridged. His method of bridging was to pick up what had been said and did not seem to fit, and, by contextualising it in a broader setting, show that it could be seen as a different emphasis rather than a contradiction. His conviction that all theological language was 'logically odd' provided an intellectual justification for believing that almost any apparent incompatability could reasonably be dealt with in this way. I think there is no doubt that this approach sometimes befogged real issues. More often, however, in my judgement it provided a useful and valid way towards at least closer mutual understanding of a religiously valuable kind.

I do not think I have ever met anyone more ready to give of his time, genuine attention, and interest to those who wanted and needed it. I think that his approach to religious thought and language (though in later years too easily and quickly applied) has a real validity. The combination of such personal, intellectual, and social concern in so human a form is for me ample evidence of a real spiritual greatness.

Results were also due to Ian Ramsey's passion for work. His disapproval of two members who absented themselves from one session in order to watch England play Germany on TV was evident. Michael Perry, the commission's secretary for most of this period, recalls:

Commission meetings began at lunch time. I had to protest in order to get discussion stopped for a tea-break—until then, tea was passed round as things went on. Break for supper; start again; go on till 10.30 or 11. Next morning, off at 9.30, coffee break if we were lucky, lunch break, and discussion till tea-time. The secretary was frenetic with activity, because he didn't have shorthand, and the chairman wanted a record for the minutes with a blow-by-blow account of the way the argument had gone. Overnight there would be a session to redraft any significant formula that might have come up during the day; and the conversation as he shaved the next morning would often be about the work laid down a few hours before. And the draft minutes would be extensively annotated by him, often for purely stylistic reasons.

What were the results of such labours under such leadership? In 1973 it is too early to say with any finality. What can, however, be seen already is that it was an achievement to have built up mutual understanding between the influential theologians who were brought together so relentlessly—at a time when many claimed that the gulf between the conservatives and the radicals was becoming unbridgeable, and that a resurgent Evangelicalism was feeling too confident to compromise. It was also an achievement to have reached the agreement needed to publish a small series of documents.

The first report, dated 10 July 1968, was on *Subscription and Assent to the 39 Articles*. The problem about these Articles, unrevised since 1571, arose because the Clerical Subscription Act of 1865 was still in force, and under it any man before being ordained, and again before assuming any clerical office, had to declare solemnly: 'I assent to the Thirty-nine Articles.... I believe the doctrine of the Church of England as therein set forth to be agreeable to the Word of God.' The Articles had also to be read in public on the first Sunday of a new incumbency. In practice most clergy in the twentieth-century Church of England disagreed with many of them, either because they thought them too Protestant or because for them knowledge, the conscience, and the whole style of theology had advanced beyond the positions adopted in the Tudor age. From time to time protests were made about the dishonesty of making ordinands and clergy 'assent' to such Articles. But they had remained one of the 'formularies' in the Church of England for two reasons: because of their historical importance as a bond of unity among Anglicans of the most diverse theological convictions, and because of the sincerity with which considerable numbers of Evangelicals still believed them to be a true echo of the Word of God.

The 1968 report expounded this situation with admirable care, and included a 'draft light revision' of the Articles: an exercise which served mainly to show that such a way of doing theology was out of place in the twentieth century. More to the point, it proposed that ordinands and clergy should no longer be required to 'assent' to the Articles or to read them publicly. Instead, they were only to 'profess my firm and sincere belief in the faith set forth in the Scriptures and in the Catholic Creeds, and my allegiance to the doctrine of the Church of England'. Before they did so, a 'Preface' was to be read: an idea first suggested by J. A. Baker late one night in a meeting at West Malling. For a time, Ian Ramsey intended it to be called a 'Contextualising Homily'; it took a specially vigorous protest from Hugh Montefiore before this title was dropped. The wording of the preface caused acute difficulty; the printing of the report had to be suspended until a last-minute change could be telephoned through. This is the proposed preface, printed here because it sums up Ian Ramsey's own loyalty to the Anglican tradition:

The Church of England is part of the Church of God, having faith in God the Father, who through Jesus Christ our only Lord and Saviour calls us into the fellowship of the Holy Spirit. This faith, uniquely shown forth in the holy Scriptures, and proclaimed in the catholic Creeds, she shares with other Christians throughout the world. She has been led by the Holy Spirit to bear a witness of her own to Christian truth in her historic formularies—the Thirty-nine Articles of Religion, and the Book of Common Prayer, and the Ordering of Bishops, Priests, and Deacons. Now, as before, she has a responsibility to maintain this witness through her preaching and worship, the writings of her scholars and teachers, the lives of her saints and confessors, and the utterances of her councils.

The report was welcomed, and now in 1973 legislation in the shape of a canon embodying its main proposal is before the General Synod. The explanation of the delay is that until the Synod's Doctrine and Worship Measure is considered and passed by Parliament (which is hoped for in the near future) doctrinal matters such as the Articles have to go before Parliament as well as before the Synod—a situation as embarrassing to most members of Parliament as it is to most members of the Church of England. Meanwhile Ian Ramsey, instead of pressing for immediate action about the Articles, turned his and the commission's energies to problems thrown up by the revision of worship—far more successful in those years than any revision of official theology. Should the dead be prayed for? Catholic-minded Anglicans were emphatic that the 'communion of saints' should be intimate despite death. It was, indeed, their tradition to pray for the repose of 'all souls of the faithful departed'. Evangelicals, however, were extremely suspicious lest such prayers, apparently implying an intermediate state between heaven and hell, should contradict the scriptural teachings that the destiny of the departed was adjudged at death. And modernists asked: why pray only for the Christian dead? It took many hours of patient discussion before the commission's members could be brought to understand each other's convictions and to agree that the departed, even those who had not been Christians, could and should be prayed for on the basis of God's will being done in them as on earth. Draft prayers were suggested which stretched Evangelical thought, although not beyond what were now seen to be the biblical limits.

The problem dealt with in another document was how additional bread and wine were to be 'consecrated' in Holy Communion, if needed when the bread and wine already included in the service had all been consumed. Once again cleavages were revealed. In the Catholic tradition the status, or even the 'substance', of the bread and wine was changed by the priest's recital of Christ's words. To Evangelicals, what mattered was the remembrance of Christ in the believer's heart. The commission united in wishing to avoid magic, and Ramsey would have preferred the new bread and wine to be placed on the altar in silence, but after a debate in the General Synod it had to be agreed that there should be a spoken formula. This was ultimately included when the 'Series Three' order of Holy Communion was issued for experimental use in 1973: 'Having given thanks to you, Father, over the bread and the cup according to the institution of your Son, Jesus Christ, who said, "Take eat: this is my body" (and/or "Drink this; this is my blood"), we pray that this bread/wine may be to us his body/blood, and be received in remembrance of him.'

Ian Ramsey did not escape the criticism levelled at the commission—and within it—for concerning itself with what seemed petty problems when the whole future of belief in God in a secular society was at stake. 'We learned to labour more and more abundantly,' John Lucas now reflects, 'to give birth to ever smaller mice.' However, the ingenuity with which these three particular problems were solved was appreciated by those responsible in ecclesiastical affairs, and before Ian Ramsey's death the commission had published a collection of essays by some of its members on deeper aspects of the Eucharist. It is possible that, had he lived, he would have been persuaded to delegate or ignore comparatively unimportant questions, and to press forward towards that theological coherence which had been Archbishop Ramsey's hope back in 1967. Certainly, in 1972 each member of the commission was asked to produce a brief statement of what he believed fundamentally. And certainly, central issues had been the subjects of Ian Ramsey's own teaching. (Had the commission studied the doctrine of the Atonement, for example, it could have had no better stimulus than the second lecture in his *Christian Discourse*.) At the end of his introduction to *Prayer and the Departed*, Ian Ramsey referred pointedly to 'traditional rivalries in areas of speculative theology, whose notoriety largely derives from their divisive power in days past'. If there was a tendency to blame the commission's absorption in minor problems on its chairman's inability to say 'no' to current pleas for help from the Church, that in itself speaks volumes about the will of the Church of England at the time to insist on the absolute priority of restating faith in God through Christ.

While a bishop, Ian Ramsey also chaired a national commission on religious education. The story of this group is best told by its secretary, Canon Alexander Wedderspoon, now of Winchester.

For over a hundred years the religious question has been a controversial issue in English education. A variety of complex problems can be sorted, basically, into two groups: those concerned with the teaching of religion in county schools and those concerned with the place of church schools in an educational system maintained by the State. By the late 1960s controversy had become acute and there were many who thought that the total exclusion of all religious teaching from maintained schools was only a matter of time. The secular humanist organizations were outspoken in their hostility; many teachers were confused about the aims and methods of religious education; some church people thought that church schools were nineteenth-century institutions; the *Honest to God* controversy advertised ferment in theology and ethics. The situation was made even more serious by the belief held by many senior administrators and educationalists that a new Education Act would be presented to Parliament in the early 1970s, thus bringing the religious question into the forefront of public debate.

This was the immediate background to the setting up of the Commission on Religious Education in 1967 under the joint sponsorship of the Church of England Board of Education and the National Society. But it was clear to us from the outset that if the selection of the right membership for the commission was important, the selection of the right chairman was crucial, and that we had only one choice.

Ian Ramsey later told us that he had resolved to refuse the chairmanship because of his existing commitments. But he decided at least to come and see us. It was a dismally wet evening and he arrived in our offices in Westminster wearing a long raincoat which he removed to reveal full episcopal dress, including gaiters. He had just come from an official occasion in the House of Lords and wryly apologized for his appearance. In a short time we were in the midst of a discussion which quickly kindled into an excitement. He accepted the chairmanship and began at once to make plans for the first meeting.

The thirty members were made up of teachers in schools, Colleges of Education, and universities, together with educational administrators and advisers. It was obvious from the start that they all had minds of their own and were certainly not going to be rushed into easy agreement. Most of the basic work was done in sub-committees, each with several coopted consultant specialists. Bishop Ramsey took the chair at all meetings of the full commission and at all meetings of the theology sub-committee. Between 1967 and 1969 this involved him in over twenty conferences of two or three days each, and regular background reading and negotiation. He was also involved in the final approval of each section of the report.

Perhaps the most outstanding feature of his chairmanship was his sheer intellectual grasp of the subjects under discussion. He was, of course, completely at ease with the most complex argument in theology, philosophy, or ethics. But he also had a sufficient fund of psychology, sociology, and commonsense to be able to discern when a specifically educational discussion was becoming precious or absurd. He could demolish an argument with force and clarity, but his rejoinder would usually include some homely and hilarious anecdote which would reduce the commission to prolonged laughter—in which any bruised feelings were at once forgotten.

It is scarcely surprising that he found it difficult to enthuse over the complex problems associated with the administration of church schools. The muddled tale of denominational bickering and reluctant compromise was, for him, a constant source of incredulity: 'it makes you wonder what they thought they were at'. He made it clear that it was his view the church schools should be allowed to continue only if good educational and pastoral reasons could be shown to justify the expense. He made it equally clear that it was not the commission's duty to manufacture reasons for the preservation of the *status quo*. This was regarded in some church circles outside the commission as a doctrine both startling and seditious, but his insistence upon a rigorously objective enquiry was fully justified.

The report *The Fourth R* was published in June 1970 and immediately became—for a report of its kind—something of a best seller. One of the reasons for this was the very careful planning of the presentation to the Press and TV. Bishop Ramsey played his full part in this, presiding over a crowded and lively Press Conference and making several broadcasts and TV appearances.

What has the Durham Report achieved? I think the answer lies in the lessening of controversy about religious education which has been apparent since the report was published. The spate of books, pamphlets and public opinion surveys which poured forth in the 1960s has largely dried up. The secular humanist organizations have turned their attention to other social issues such as the abortion controversy. The educationalists have been more concerned with the content and method of religious education rather than with disputes about basic policy. There has been a widespread acceptance of the report as a document which sets out, fairly and sensitively, the educational justification for the teaching of religion in schools. It has helped to demonstrate that the debate about religious education is essentially a serious educational question and not merely a tussle between some good people called Christians and some wicked people called atheists. In the negotiations leading up to a new Education Act it is reasonable to hope that the religious issue will be discussed with much deeper and more intelligent understanding.

Within the Church of England, one of the results has been the publication of a clear and challenging report by a commission chaired by the Bishop of Carlisle which makes some very radical recommendations about the future of the educational work of the dioceses. But perhaps the most important result is that the report has found its way on to the reading lists of students all over Britain. To some extent it has also been influential in the thinking going on about this subject elsewhere in the world. It is more than just a tract for the times and its influence may well not become fully apparent until the 1980s.

Another long-felt concern reached a fresh expression when his friend, the Roman Catholic theologian Bishop B. C. Butler, persuaded him to join the Executive Committee of the Social Morality Council in 1968. The chairman was H. J. Blackham, formerly Director of the British Humanist Association. Ramsey threw himself into the residential meetings held privately each year to discuss fundamental personal values; into a national project to encourage moral education in the schools; and into other activities which the religious and the secular could share equally in the service of society.

He became Chairman of the Governors of William Temple College in 1967. At that stage it was housed in the old Rectory at Rugby, and with Mollie Batten as Principal it specialized in two activities: short courses where people in industry (both unions and management) could listen and talk through their common problems, and longer courses for laymen (mainly women) wanting a serious training in theology, particularly in the relations between theology and disciplines such as sociology. Ramsey had already paid many visits to the college for discussions and Governors' meetings, but it turned out that the most difficult problem in his time as chairman (when Len Tyler was Principal) was financial. In the end the Rugby buildings were sold and the college was put under the wing of Manchester University. One of Ramsey's last acts was to preside over the appointment of his friend and colleague from Oxford days, David Jenkins, as Principal of William Temple College in Manchester.

He had played an enthusiastic part in the creation of the Institute of Religion and Medicine in 1964, bringing together clergy, doctors, and others in the study of health and healing in ways which would be sound both medically and theologically. He became the vice-chairman of its council in 1966 and its chairman in 1971. Hugh Melinsky writes: 'He gave the Institute the highest priority among his manifold engagements and its successful growth over eight years owed a great deal to Ian's care, zeal, wisdom, and wide range of contacts. Typical of his enthusiasm was a recent visit to Norwich when he preached to a cathedral full of doctors and nurses for the bicentenary of the Norfolk and Norwich Hospital; then lectured in the evening at a three-hour seminar of the Norfolk and Norwich Theological Society on "Abortion and Euthanasia", and had to be driven to Peterborough that night so that he could catch a train the next morning to Durham.' He accepted many invitations to do this kind of thing, and the extent of the activities of this Institute may be gauged from the fact that by the end of 1972 it listed almost forty secretaries of groups or areas throughout Britain. He wrote careful prefaces to the two volumes of essays which it sponsored on *Religion and Medicine*.

Partly because of this involvement, and partly because of the respect in which fellow-members of the group which produced *Science and Personality* held him, he was accorded the rare distinction of giving the inaugural lecture of the conference of the British Medical Association in Cyprus in April 1972. In the end this had to be read for him because he was in hospital, but it had been prepared elaborately and was later printed.[1] It ranged over moral problems facing the medical profession, but attracted most attention by its discussion of the techniques and moral dilemmas involved in the prolongation of life by artificial means. When is a person who seems dead to the layman really dead? Should doctors always attempt to keep people alive when they possibly can? Ramsey's detailed and uninhibited probing of such questions startled anyone who still regarded him as just a bishop, but of even greater interest as one looks back is the principle: 'the Christian certainly will not be motivated by the supposition that death is at all costs something to be avoided'.

Ramsey said that to a Christian 'death is of all events the one in which the grace of God is to be found. In all the stark loneliness of death, confronted by the abyss of death, we are to prove pre-

[1] For example, in the *Bishoprick* for August 1972.

eminently God's transforming power. In that sense death is the
gate to life eternal ... something natural and inevitable for which
we not only can but must prepare, the gateway through which we
are to move to that fruition, that fulfilment, which is God's purpose
for us.'

His death came on 6 October 1972, at the age of fifty-seven. He
had spent the day in the chair of a committee at Broadcasting
House; it was his first journey to London alone on 'business as
usual' since his severe heart attack on Easter Eve. During much of
the intervening period, he had been quietly convalescent in Auckland Castle or away in the Lake District with his wife. Margaret
Ramsey recalls with gratitude that all through this summer they
were together in a leisure greater than they had known since the
earliest years of their married life. These were months leaving
behind many good memories. On his last day in Durham he
visited a school; curiously, it was his first and only experience of
teaching in a classroom. One boy asked with an innocent curiosity,
when the bishop had talked about God: 'Sir, are you afraid to
die?' The reply 'no' was honest.

John Lang, Head of Religious Broadcasting at the BBC, writes:

When in 1970 the BBC and the Independent Television (now Broadcasting) Authority were looking for a successor to the Bishop of Bristol as
Chairman of the Central Religious Advisory Committee, no-one had
any doubt that Ian Ramsey would be a first-class man for the job. The
only worry was whether it was right to ask him in view of his heavy
burden of duties inside and outside the diocese of Durham. His warm
response to an informal approach by Penry Jones, the Head of Religious
Broadcasting, settled the matter and the Chairman of the BBC sent him
a formal invitation.

In the light of all that followed his reply is interesting. Characteristically it was written in his own hand, probably in a train.

My dear Lord Hill,
    I am grateful for your letter of July 22nd, and honoured by this
invitation to become Chairman of CRAC. I have pondered the matter
very carefully, not least in relation to what you know are my other
weighty commitments, and I am grateful to you for giving me the
details you did. In the end my interest in this field, and my convictions
about the significance of religious broadcasting, have pointed me to

acceptance, and I must shed what I can of what has less priority. I hope I shall justify your trust, and that of those you have consulted.

Kindest regards,

Yours sincerely,

IAN DUNELM

Sydney Evans, Dean of King's College, London, told me after Ian Ramsey's death that he had read of this appointment with sorrow. Surely this was a job someone else could have done, leaving Ian to do what only he could do. But the fact is that though the chairmanship of CRAC does not take up much time it does require substantial skill. The committee includes members of all the main churches in the country and represents many different opinions within them. Further, it advises both the broadcasting authorities and has to walk delicately between them. Finally it deals directly with senior professional broad-casters who know their jobs thoroughly. They are friendly but also formidable.

The committee has been fortunate in its chairmen, beginning as far back as 1923 with Cyril Garbett, then Bishop of Southwark. But none has come to it with greater prestige than Ian Ramsey, nor perhaps managed it better. His first meeting was on 18 March 1971 and it was an exceptionally difficult one. The Central Religious Advisory Committee not only advises the BBC on religious policy but also the IBA. Normally it keeps the business of the two broadcasting authorities entirely separate, but occasionally this is not possible. Ian Ramsey's first meeting was one such occasion. The subject was the future of the so-called 'Closed Period' (the time between 6.15 and 7.25 pm on Sunday evenings which is normally given over to religious television). There was substantial disagreement on the subject among the committee members and the two broadcasting organizations had divergent views. My own recollection is that Ian Ramsey floundered as chairman for about ten minutes before suddenly learning to swim. By the end of the day he chaired four meetings in one. CRAC had talked to the BBC alone and to the IBA alone. It had met by itself and finally it faced the BBC and the IBA together. It had achieved unanimity in its advice and persuaded the broadcasters it was right.

One important outcome of this meeting was the setting up of a small working party on the committee's own activities which met, until his first illness, under Ian Ramsey's own chairmanship and afterwards under that of Dr. Horace Walker. It submitted its final report at the bishop's last meeting and its recommendations are even now being put into effect.

That last meeting was also the last day of Ian Ramsey's life. When it was over he asked me if he could stay behind in the Council Chamber to do some work before going home. A few minutes later Mr. F. L. Tomlinson went into the room to clear up after the meeting. He greeted the bishop, who began to reply but suddenly fell forward across the table. Mr. Tomlinson got medical help with the utmost speed, first a nurse and then the ambulance. I got back from my office as the bishop was being carried, unconscious, out of Broadcasting House. I went with him to the Middlesex Hospital fearing he might already be dead. In fact he was not and the waiting doctors at first got a slight reaction from his heart. It was a false hope, however, and a quarter of an hour later I was told he had died.

It was astonishing to me, looking at the records, that Ian Ramsey only chaired three meetings of CRAC. He made a vivid impact on those who had dealings with him and managed to be many things to many people. Somehow he always found time, and good counsel, for those seeking his advice. He won respect and affection everywhere. One of our waitresses wept after his death because a few hours before she had such a friendly conversation with him about slimming. Yet he could without any show of force dominate a meeting of powerful people. He was small in stature but large in spirit.

Such was the work to which Ian Ramsey gave his life. It is for the reader to decide whether the work was worth doing, and whether it is worth continuing.

Appendix

IAN RAMSEY

*An Address at the Memorial Service
in St. Margaret's, Westminster,
on Friday 17 November, 1972,
by Michael Ramsey, Archbishop of Canterbury,
formerly Bishop of Durham*

THREE of Durham's great bishops were buried in the lovely medieval chapel of Auckland Castle: Cosin, Lightfoot, Westcott; and it is fitting that the ashes of Ian Ramsey are to lie near to them. It will not be surprising if history comes to remember Brooke Foss Westcott and Ian Ramsey as the two bishops who made the biggest impact upon the Durham community.

It is never easy to speak about a dear friend or a great man, and it is doubly hard to speak about one who was both. I have known other men who had something of Ian's winning warmth of heart and others who had Ian's liveliness of mind; but I have never known one in whom the warm heart and the lively mind were so completely of one piece. That was the secret of his influence as a theologian. He cared intensely that theology should listen to other disciplines if it is to have something intelligible to say in the contemporary scene. He cared no less that those who speak about Christian faith should do so with sensitivity to the many who find faith hard or incredible. These gifts made Ian Ramsey nearly unique amongst the theologians of our time in winning the attention and respect of people trained in other kinds of mental discipline. And for Ian this outreach on the frontiers of faith could never be an intellectual process alone. It meant outgoing friendship with people of many professions, a ceaseless engagement of heart and mind alike, a ceaseless giving of himself.

So when Ian left the academic life of Oxford for the very different tasks of a Bishop of Durham there was, for all the vast change of scene, a striking continuity of work and character. In Durham it was quickly apparent that he cared greatly about the community and its problems and was thinking vigorously about them. Those who worked in the mines and the shipyards, trades-unionists and managers alike, those who took part in local government or education or medicine or the social services, saw in the bishop one who understood and cared, with a concern for people as well as for ideas and causes. So there was a renewal in a fresh form of the historic link between the see of Durham and the community, for Ian had a sense of the past as well as the present, and he was never happier than when he welcomed crowds of visitors to the bishop's historic home and showed them the memorials of his great predecessors.

Inevitably Ian Ramsey's leadership was reaching far beyond his own diocese. The work of the Doctrine Commission, the production of the report on education entitled *The Fourth R*, the work of other groups of his own creation, a succession of speeches in the House of Lords made with the weight of considerable knowledge —amid all this his impact as a Christian leader was growing, and it was a leadership of a kind which no one else could give. But a frightening problem began to appear.

Is it possible for one man to lead the pastoral work of a diocese with its outreach to the community and at the same time to be taking part in national affairs and at the same time also to conserve the work of study, reading, thought, and teaching? Not many bishops have tried to combine these three roles at once, and those who have tried know that survival is only possible if there is a rigorous discipline in excluding things which do not matter and limiting painfully the things which do. Alas, it was impossible for Ian to admit the advice and experience of those who know something of the problem, because it had become a deep and inseparable part of his character never to say 'no'. And in the office which he held never to say 'no' means before long to lose the power of discrimination and to be living in a whirl of mental and physical movement. The whirl became the whirlwind which swept Ian, like Elijah of old, to Paradise.

Yet perhaps if it were otherwise Ian would not be Ian. Perhaps the saying of 'no' to any request of a fellow human being and the planning of priorities for himself were impossible for one to whom any incidental encounter, any person met, could be a thrilling disclosure, a bursting forth of one of God's secrets. Such was the man, with mind and heart ceaselessly engaged with people and ceaselessly engaged with truth and ready for truth to break out anywhere in a blaze of glory. That was the Ian God gave to us, and we are thanking God today for one of the best of his gifts that we have known, a gift not like any other. Our loving prayers surround Ian's brave family at this time, and for Ian we pray that he will now have the vision which our Saviour promised to the pure in heart.